BY LYZ LENZ

This American Ex-Wife: How I Ended My Marriage
and Started My Life

God Land: A Story of Faith, Loss, and Renewal
in Middle America

Belabored: A Vindication of the Rights
of Pregnant Women

THIS AMERICAN EX-WIFE

THIS AMERICAN EX-WIFE

How I Ended My Marriage and Started My Life

LYZ LENZ

CROWN
NEW YORK

Copyright © 2024 by E Claire Enterprises LLC

Published in the United States by Crown, an imprint of Crown Publishing
Group, a division of Penguin Random House LLC, New York.

CROWN and the Crown colophon are registered trademarks of
Penguin Random House LLC.

Hardback ISBN 978-0-593-24112-7
Ebook ISBN 978-0-593-44268-5

Printed in the United States of America on acid-free paper

crownpublishing.com

2 4 6 8 9 7 5 3

Editor: Libby Burton
Editorial assistants: Aubrey Martinson and Cierra Hinckson
Production editor: Mark Birkey
Text designer: Susan Turner
Production manager: Linnea Knollmueller
Managing editors: Allison Fox and Sally Franklin
Copy editor: Michelle Daniel
Publicist: Bree Martinez
Marketer: Melissa Esner

*For all of my sisters: the ones I shared a womb with
and the ones I share the world with*

I desire my freedom above all else in the world
and I am justified in seeking it.

—Blanche Molineux

CONTENTS

THIS AMERICAN EX-WIFE

The End

My marriage ended on a Monday.

I walked into my house at one A.M., having just completed a sixteen-hour round research trip to Indiana in twenty-four hours. I was trying to write my first book while raising a four-year-old and a two-year old, with little childcare, and the care I did have was cobbled together Rube Goldberg–style from friends and a part-time day care program at a church. I opened the back door and stepped over the usual pile of shoes and coats into the kitchen. I flipped on the light and saw a trash bag on the floor, spilling the detritus of my life: Go-GURT wrappers, tissues, plastic plates, Goldfish crackers, damp napkins, orange peels, dried chunks of cheese, and a broken toy from a fast food chain.

This had happened so many times before. My husband emptied the trash and set the full bag on the bench in the breakfast nook. He'd take it out in the morning, he'd tell himself. Much like the myth of leaving the dishes to soak so he could wash them the next day. Perhaps the greatest trick a husband has ever played was convincing himself (and his wife) that he'd get to a chore the next day.

I imagined the bag sitting there as he watched *Star Trek*, slowly wobbling on the edge of the bench, until, with a wet slap, it hit the floor. Maybe he never heard it. He'd never really had to pay attention like that—to the left-behind crumbs, the sticky spots on the floor. But to me, an older daughter of eight children and now a mother, those small messes were the only things I saw.

I had spent the eleven years of our marriage trying to get him to see that the dishwasher drain didn't clean itself and the socks didn't crawl out of the laundry and find their own mates and put themselves in his drawer. I wanted him to notice. I wanted him to see these small labors.

Sometimes I calmly requested *Please just take the trash outside*. Other times, I refused to clean it up. Sometimes I raged. Often, he would be irritated and say he forgot and put off the chore again. Once, in the first year of our marriage, I'd let the bag sit for an entire week before the smell of rotting garbage filled the kitchen. I was the first one who blinked in that game of chicken, hauling it out and then cleaning up the wet mark the bag had left on the wooden bench. The stain remains there.

Once, in a fight, my husband said that each chore was simply a chore and just that. He was criticizing my propensity to talk not just about the one trash bag on the floor but all the trash bags that had ever fallen. These were minor things, he argued. Just trash. Not such a big deal. It's easy to see chores as a one-off when they are not the bulk of your life. When your work and leisure aren't woven among the laundry, the dishes, the vacuuming, and the grocery shopping. When you aren't wondering whether there is enough dish soap or if you have enough potatoes for dinner. Standing there in the kitchen that early Monday morning, I was exhausted. Marriage, it seemed, was this: the eternal return of trash on my floor.

Nietzsche's idea of eternal return argues that all events in time and space occur over and over and will continue to occur infinitely—as in marriage. People grow and change, yes. But not that much. In marriage, you have the same arguments over and over. *As long as you both shall live.* My husband was right. I could never just see a pile of trash. I saw all the past piles, and on that morning I saw all the future piles, too. I saw an eternity of trash piles. *This is my life. This will always be my life.* The moment I'd said "I do," I'd entered a time continuum, where trash on the floor would always happen. And I would always be cleaning it up. And nothing I could do, no amount of couples therapy or list making, could stop the inevitable tumble and wet splat.

Looking at the mess, I began to do the mental math—what did I have the energy for? Wiping the floor or fighting? Add those factors together, solve for trash on the floor. That morning, the solution was to pick it up.

Later, I went to bed and dreamed I was drowning. I woke up three hours later, at five A.M., to my two-year-old son patting my cheeks. My son vehemently believed five A.M. was the appropriate time to wake up. Most mornings I would sit with him watching *Curious George,* drinking coffee, and reading the news on my phone, while he snuggled into the corner of the couch with his little blankie rubbing against his cheeks.

That morning, my body vibrated with exhaustion, but I didn't have time for coffee and *Curious George.* The house cleaner (a lovely woman from my church who'd offered to help me when she'd asked me how I was doing, and I broke out into sobs) was coming that day, and I had to clean up all the mess that had accumulated while I was gone.

The truth about accepting help is that it requires asking for it and coordinating it and paying for it, emotionally and financially. Financially, I took on extra freelance work to pay for housecleaning because it wasn't in the budget. Emotionally, I dealt with my husband's heavy sighs when he'd walk into a professionally cleaned home, and his angry silences that would fill the space between us until I'd explained I'd sold a little article to pay for it. It didn't come out of the shared checking account. Sometimes my husband would say, "If you want help just ask," and I would wave my arms around me like someone drowning. "Just look!" I'd say. "This is all a cry for help." But truthfully, I didn't want help. I was grateful for it, sure. What I wanted was an equal partner.

My husband came downstairs at seven-fifty to pack his lunch and leave for work.

"There was trash all over the floor," I said.

He rolled his eyes.

"The point is, there was a large pile of trash I had to wade through when I came home."

"You are welcome for watching the kids."

There are moments where couples teeter on the edge of a fight. Just one look, one word, will push you over into the chasm of fury. I let us rest on that edge that morning. My world already felt so fragile. Donald Trump had been elected ten months before. I had not voted for him, but my husband had. It was the end of August now and we were in couples therapy every week, where we discussed his attitude toward my career (bad, he didn't like it and wanted me to just write mystery novels), and my attitude toward his attitude (bad, I didn't like it and I wanted him to just vacuum the rug for once, and never in my life had I written a mystery novel), and all the things I had lost in the marriage.

And I *was* losing things. The entire time we'd been together, I seemed to slough off items—mugs, chambray shirts, small books, larger books. We'd been married for so long, eleven years at that point, that I had just assumed it was me. This was just who I was. He'd often refer to my absent-mindedness, joking that I'd mislay my head if it wasn't attached to my neck. But that spring, while cleaning out the house for a garage sale, in the musty basement crawl space behind the worthless china my mean grandma had bequeathed me and the boxes of wedding decorations, I'd found everything I had lost.

I was in purge mode, occasionally shouting to my kids not to fight over who got to play with the little mop I'd bought to teach them about cleaning but that they were using to sword fight, when I reached for a box and opened it up. Inside was everything I thought I had lost. Mugs, shirts, and books. For the entirety of my marriage, my husband had been taking things of mine he didn't like and hiding them in this box in the basement.

The legend of Bluebeard tells the story of a man who weds women, murders them, and hides their bodies in a room. His most recent wife, newly wed and brought to live in his castle, is given the keys and told she can explore everywhere in her new home except one room. When Bluebeard leaves to go on a trip, her curiosity takes over and she opens the door to the forbidden room and sees, there on the floor, the bodies of the wives who have come before her. She drops the key, which becomes stained with their blood, and she cannot wash it off. Bluebeard returns and sees the blood on the key and knows that she knows the truth. In some versions of the story, the bride is saved from death by her siblings. In others, she dies but is restored to life. And in others, she is murdered and joins the collection of bodies. It's similar to the story of the Garden of Eden. A woman given everything is told to not do one thing, not to eat of the forbidden fruit. She does, and she learns the truth about life and death. Knowing, those stories tell us, is worse than blissful ignorance.

Opening that box felt like opening the door to Bluebeard's room. Inside of it were dead versions of myself. A mug that read WRITE LIKE A MOTHERFUCKER, two chambray button-up shirts that I had loved to wear while nursing, my copy of *Madame Bovary,* a mug with the faces of famous Democrats on them, a little book of conversation starters that I'd bought when we were dating as a way to get him to open up. *What would you do with a million dollars? If you could have one superpower what would it be? What would you do if you discovered the person you love has been hiding your things away for your entire marriage?*

I brought the box upstairs and put it on the counter. And then, because it was a warm day, I set up the small plastic pool for the kids and fed them Popsicles until dinnertime. It felt like another woman was doing all those things. Another woman tickling her daughter. Another woman telling her son to just pee in the bushes, it was fine. The real woman was somewhere inside me, asking herself what else she had lost. What else was she missing that she didn't even know was gone?

When my husband came home, I pointed to the box. Our kids clamored around him, hugging him, welcoming him home.

"What is this?" I asked.

He turned to hug the kids and, without looking me in the eye, asked what was for dinner.

I couldn't find the words to speak. I went upstairs and sat in the bedroom with the door closed. Not knowing whether to scream or cry. Eventually, I did what I normally did. I went downstairs and made dinner. I should have left. I should have run out the door. But I wouldn't do that for six more months. I wanted to make it work. I wasn't a quitter.

For the next four months, we went to couples therapy once a week, rehashing our marriage, every fight, every moment, every stolen item, every lost dream. I told the therapist about the hidden box.

He hid them, he told the therapist, because he didn't like them, and what was the big deal? It was just stuff.

She made him promise not to do it again.

But I don't think either one of them really understood that what had been taken from me wasn't just my mugs, but my entire sense of self.

I had not wanted to move to Iowa. He'd gotten his dream job as an engineer in Cedar Rapids. I had graduated with an English degree and a Russian minor. So I'd gone along with him because any job I was offered would never pay as much. But he promised that someday soon we would move. Someday soon we would go somewhere where there were jobs for writers. But it had been eleven years and we'd had kids and that someday soon had never come.

Research shows that couples are more likely to move for the man's career rather than the woman's. In 2014, a study argued that couples moved because women had a propensity to take more flexible jobs. With the demands of home and childcare still falling primarily upon the shoulders of women, of course women have to be more flexible. But do men just take location-stable jobs because they like them? Or has it never occurred to them to look for something more flexible because they don't need to bend and break themselves for family and marriage?

Eve Rodsky, the author of *Fair Play*, pointed out that the very idea of a woman's job being more flexible is a myth. "We found in our studies that if a woman is a lawyer and a man's a doctor, she says her job is more flexible," she notes. "If you flip it and she's the doctor and he's the lawyer, guess what?

She says her job is more flexible. There's just such a different expectation over how women are supposed to use their time that we become so conditioned to spending our time in service of others that we give away our most valuable currency, our time, for free." Was my job really more flexible, or was it just perceived as flexible because I was the female partner?

I'd been raised in a world that said women could do anything, and I'd imagined a life so different from that of my mother's, which had been defined by children and housework—but here I was. No amount of education had helped me escape this. No jobs. No self-help books. No amount of therapy had helped me avoid the inevitable: cleaning up the trash on the floor of the kitchen at midnight.

When we talk about the beginning of the end of a marriage, there is rarely just one moment that breaks everything apart. There are often several small stressors that you don't even notice until everything is shattered.

In spring 2016, I received an email from a publisher who read an article I wrote on religion and politics in Middle America and wanted to know if I was interested in turning it into a book. I'd been trying to get publishers interested in my writing for years without much success. I even had a literary agent, but she hadn't been able to sell the book I had written. So when this offer came, I thought this was my chance, and I threw everything into that project. But the more the book came together, the more my life fell apart.

Studies show that when women advance in their careers

they are more likely to get a divorce, and so are female bread-winners. One 2020 study specifically analyzed women in the European Union who have more income parity than American women and more of a social safety net. It wasn't the lack of social support that made these women divorce; it was the lack of relational support. One of the study's authors, Johanna Rickne, a professor at the University of Stockholm, pointed out that men are used to being asked to fill the gap in domestic duties but not used to being asked to take on more than that. It is "still seen as quite unusual for men to be the main supportive spouse in someone else's career," said Rickne. Ask for fifty-fifty, and that is okay. Ask for fifty-one-forty-nine, and the marriage falls apart. In her book *The Light We Carry,* Michelle Obama writes that marriage is not a scale, but an abacus. A sliding measure. It's dynamic and ever-changing. But so often for wives, the measure breaks when we ask for the scale to slide in our favor.

Charlotte Ljung, a Swedish CEO of a bed and furniture group, is quoted in the study, noting, "It is also the power perception—who wears the pants, who brings in more money. Men today often find it intriguing in the beginning and want to be seen to support you and root for you—and I think that is a very positive thing—but I think a few steps down the line, when reality kicks in, it can be more difficult for men to deal with." So often, successful women are portrayed as harried and unable to focus on their homes and families. In *The Devil Wears Prada,* Meryl Streep plays a successful magazine editor, Miranda Priestly, whose overlooked husband leaves her. As Stanley Tucci's character, Nigel, opines to Anne Hathaway, who plays Streep's beleaguered assistant, "Let me know when your whole life goes up in smoke. Means it's time for a promotion." We are supposed to believe that this careerism is what ruins marriages. But men have careers and families all the time. They're able to do this because they have a partner at home supporting them. Essentially, it's not the time commitment and stress of success that breaks up these marriages; it's the husband's resentment about the time commitment and stress that breaks up the marriage.

And it was true for me. The closer I came to achieving my dreams, the more my home life fell apart. And it wasn't because I wasn't getting everything done. I was still cooking, cleaning, grocery shopping, and writing my book. But I was asking for more. Not a lot, just a little more. Maybe he brought home takeout once a week? Maybe he vacuumed the floors once in a while? Maybe he took the kids grocery shopping? Maybe he planned the meals? I would have settled for the scraps of his efforts. But he'd vacuum once and never do it again. Grocery shop once and complain that it was too hard to do with the kids. After eleven years of marriage, the weight of our lives slid toward him, and the whole marriage broke.

As I was working on the book, my husband suggested we have a third child. He brought it up in therapy one day that summer when I was in the middle of research and writing. Maybe I could quit writing for a while? he suggested. Maybe I could just write a nice little novel and write it at night after the kids were in bed. And we could have another kid. Wouldn't I be less stressed out?

I stared at him in disbelief. My dream was just within my reach, and he wanted me to give it up? I turned to the therapist, and she placidly asked, "What are you feeling right now?"

I imagined slapping them both in the face and then kicking the door down and running down the street.

"I feel angry, Janice. Really fucking angry."

It soon became clear I could be successful or I could be married. We had been in therapy on and off for a few years. But that summer, we were in therapy once a week. I would ask for help, and he would ask me to do less writing—giving up what I'd accomplished. We talked about this in therapy. We talked about everything in therapy. But once we left the office, him driving away to work and me driving back home, we didn't speak of anything of substance. We discussed the children, but once they went to bed, we'd sit in silence, often watching *Star Trek,* which he'd turn on while I did the dishes or caught up on email.

I once read in an article that Joan Didion and John Dunne had once considered splitting up but had gone to Hawaii instead. In therapy, I asked to go to Florida. We needed time together. We needed time away. Maybe the Didion solution was the answer.

"Vacations are too expensive," he said. "How about something else?" And he turned to me and the therapist to come up with ideas.

"How about a shared activity, like a puzzle?" the therapist suggested. One time, I'd said I liked puzzles in therapy. One time. And now here we were, using it as the splint to reset our broken lives.

I'd wanted Hawaii, I would have settled for Florida, and what I got was a five-thousand-piece puzzle with a picture of the ocean. And the most offensive part was that the metaphor was so contrived.

"Individuals," Milan Kundera writes, "organize their lives according to the laws of beauty, even in times of greatest distress." What he meant was that we are always looking for symbols and signs to create meaning, where there are none. To find a metaphor where there is only a floor of blue puzzle pieces.

I thought about how I had constructed meaning in the beginning of our relationship. Carole King's "So Far Away" for our long-distance courtship. "When You Say Nothing at All" to make narrative sense of his prolonged silences. A little alien doll he had won at a county fair and handed to me, telling me I was "weird like an alien." Wasn't that charming? And I'd laughed and I kept it. I kept all of those things he gave me: a gold heart necklace, the letters he wrote in college, all of the little bits of evidence that meant we were supposed to be together. On their own, they were just things, but when you put them together they meant we were in love.

Now, we had a puzzle. If we finished it, we'd piece together our marriage. If we didn't, we'd always be a broken picture. (I told you the metaphor was contrived.) So, every night, for that long summer of 2017, I'd come downstairs after rocking my toddler son to sleep. My husband would already be on the floor with the puzzle mat rolled out, slowly putting together the pieces, *Star Trek* on in the background. I sat next to him. I would sort, making a system—edges first, then organize by color and consistency. If you could be organized, a puzzle was something you could lose yourself in, the colors, the patterns, the shapes, the infinite pleasure of making everything fit.

But there were so many pieces, and we never talked. All those tiny bits of blue reminding me of the vacation I was not going to get. Until one day, I couldn't do it anymore. I walked down the stairs, and stepped over the puzzle mat, sat on the couch, and changed the TV show from *Star Trek* to *Damages,* the show where Glenn Close plays an evil murdering lawyer. We never finished the puzzle.

I was the one who broke. I want to make that clear. If I hadn't, we might still be together. This book wouldn't exist. Much of my work wouldn't exist. But my marriage would. And maybe we'd reach the end of our lives and have happy, peaceful moments. And our children might idolize what we had, not knowing, never knowing, how much it cost me. In the 1996 remake of the movie *101 Dalmatians,* Cruella de Vil tells Anita Darling, "More good women have been lost to marriage than to war, famine, disease, and disaster. You have talent, darling. Don't squander it." It's true. Women are taught that it is noble to lose themselves inside their marriage. To give up everything for home and children, even themselves. I often wonder how many stories, how many scientific breakthroughs, how many plays, musical scores, and innovations, have been tossed onto the pyre of human marriage.

In Henrik Ibsen's play *A Doll's House*, the husband looks at his wife and tells her, "Before all else you are a wife and mother." And she replies, "I don't believe that any longer. I believe that before all else I am a reasonable human being just as you are—or, at all events, that I must try and become one." That play was written in 1879, but the words still seem radical today. Our television shows and movies are filled with grizzled men, heroes, choosing their careers over their families, because these careers, these professions, will save the world. How rare is it to see women doing this and still being allowed to be the heroes of the story? I am not saying that the work I have done and will do is so incredible that it justifies everything, but I am saying it doesn't have to. I don't have to win a Nobel Prize or be a heart surgeon for my life, my ambition, and my happiness to be worth fighting for.

But women and their work have always been disposable. During WWII, as men fought overseas, women were urged to enter the workforce, to produce the machines of war. The government provided free universal childcare to the women who worked (with the exception of women of color) to encourage them to have careers. They were celebrated as heroes. Rosie the Riveters making America great. But the moment the war was over, the childcare program ended. Women were forced back to the home. Their work was valued only when it replaced that of dying men. The moment the surviving men came home, women were expected to become invisible again.

In 2020, when pandemic shutdowns kept children at home, the burden fell on mothers, who had no options, no childcare, no help, and were forced out of the workforce. While airlines and banks received bailouts, families received only childcare tax credits, which were ended in 2022. Despite the fact that these tax credits were helping to end child poverty, and banks continued to receive bailouts, the help disappeared. The labor of women once again rendered invisible. The question is not why women break, it's how they ever hold it together.

My marriage ended on a Monday. Early that morning, I came home and found the trash on the floor. But it wasn't the trash on the floor that finally broke me. If the trash had driven me up to the edge of the cliff, the missing DRINK UP, WITCHES! sign pushed me over.

After dropping the kids off at school, I walked through the dining room, making sure the remnants of breakfast were cleaned up. I saw that something was missing—a little wooden sign I displayed on the antique hutch in the dining room that read DRINK UP, WITCHES!

The sign itself was silly. Something purchased on a whim from Target. I am, after all, an aging white mother in the Midwest, who unironically loves Starbucks. I love puns about drinking and being a witch. And one day I'd bought the sign for three dollars and tucked it into a little corner of the dining room. Now it was missing. After that whole summer, after that stupid puzzle, after all his promises in therapy to never hide my things again, that sign, that stupid little sign that brought me so much joy, was gone. I knew he'd taken it. And he'd taken it because he didn't like it. He didn't like me.

I stood in the dining room. The house was silent. I stared at the deep green walls, which I'd painted just days before my son was born. The buzz of my early morning coffee was wearing off and my body was tired. More tired than I had ever remembered being, even in the early exhaustion-tunnel days when I had a two-year-old and a newborn and my nipples bled.

If before I had felt like I was trying to stop my life from teetering off the edge, this was the moment I surrendered to it. I felt like I was falling, and so I fell. Whatever brokenness waited for me, I suddenly wanted. Because this wholeness, this version of home, marriage, and family, would ruin me.

"I quit," I said out loud, and only the house heard me.

Nearly 70 percent of divorces are initiated by women—women who are tired, fed up, exhausted, no longer in love. Women who are unhappy. Some of their breaking moments are quiet. Some are loud. They are simple and they are profound. Often these women are dismissed as a lone madwoman, unable to cope. They are problems for a therapist and a self-help book to solve. Certainly not a political crisis. But I don't think that's true. After I left my marriage, I began to talk to hundreds of women about their moment of breaking. It happened almost by accident. When you divorce, women like to tell you about their own problems, their own marriages; they tell you of the frustrations that lay behind their own happily constructed homes and smiling holiday cards. "Should I get divorced?" they ask in whispers, in DMs, in Facebook messages, in coffee shops. "How do you know when it's time to go?" They all want to know.

I soon realized I wasn't alone. My story wasn't compelling or unique; I was simply one of hundreds of thousands of women who saw their lives falling apart from the common-place pressures of society and patriarchy. It wasn't violent abuse. It wasn't another woman. It was trash on the floor, sticky counters, and please please please clean the bath-room, over and over, until I couldn't do it anymore. And maybe I could have. Maybe I could have just given up and been miserable for a few years until our children were older. But I didn't want to. I didn't want to waste my one wild and precious life telling a grown man where to find the ketchup in the fridge. What was compelling about my marriage wasn't its evils or its villains, but its commonplace horror.

And what I realized after talking to these women was how many of us there were standing outside of this patriar-chal paradise of marriage—women who'd broken, and then forged new lives for ourselves, new ways of loving and living, and how we had been doing this for centuries. We didn't want a how-to book to fix these bad and broken relation-ships. We didn't want advice on how to get back out there and find new love. What we wanted was to be free.

I noticed patterns, too—these weren't just stories of women falling out of love, but of a political and cultural and romantic institution that asks too much of wives and moth-ers and gives too little in return. As one mother of four, who runs her own small business, stated, "I'm a divorced single mom. Leaving my husband didn't increase my workload. He wasn't doing much. My workload is the same, but I have more peace now."

These are not the rantings of bitter women. Well, they are sometimes bitter, but when did being bitter imply that women weren't telling the truth? Why does being bitter disqualify a woman's voice? I listened as the stories piled up one after another. The whisper network of women who'd broken their lives apart and found freedom and happiness. The women who had left the failed utopia of marriage and were living on the outside of Eden, speaking a truth only they knew—it was better out here. There were better ways to live.

So often, when women reach milestones in our lives (marriage, babies, menopause), we reflect on what we wish we would have been told. This book is that telling. I wanted the voices of these Liliths to whisper to Eve before it was too late. I wanted the women in Bluebeard's room to rise from the dead and scream. This is my story, but it's the story of so many women, looking at the sliding scale of their relational abacus and wondering when the balance will tip in their favor. When it's one woman breaking, it's an individual problem. But when it's more than one woman, it's a societal problem.

These breaking moments are all small, such as discovering a witch sign is missing. But they are all profound. My friend Anna told me that the moment she knew her marriage was over was when her ex told her he didn't like feta on his omelet. They'd had a huge fight the night before and had gone to bed exhausted from yelling. But when they woke up, Anna was determined to set things right. While her husband slept, she made brunch for the two of them. When he woke up, he stumbled into the kitchen and poked the omelets with his fingers.

"Feta?" he said. "You know I don't like feta."

Anna dumped the whole meal in the trash and went for

a walk. When she came back, she knew the marriage was over.

On Twitter a woman told me she knew her marriage was over when she saw her husband kick their dog. Another woman wrote to tell me that she knew when her ex took a painting of calligraphic art she had purchased from Turkey off the wall so he could hang it in his office. Another woman told me that it was when she went into her ten-month-old son's room to hold him after her husband had hit her. Holding her son, with bruises forming on her body, she knew she would leave the next day.

The moment people knew their marriage was over ranges from the simple ("I saw him in a robe and realized I wasn't comfortable enough around him anymore to wear a robe in my own home") to the violent ("He left a gun on the table"). Many men reply to say they were stunned ("One day I woke up, she was gone, and money was missing"). Other men report small betrayals. ("I told her I wanted to go to therapy. She wished me luck finding one. I realized I was on my own then.") And then the cheating—always the cheating. What struck me was that women seemed to know the end was coming, while men simply seemed surprised by it. One man told me he knew only when she didn't come home one day and was served with papers three months later.

Because it is overwhelmingly the wives who initiate divorce, and because the weight of social, cultural, and political bias is stacked against the experience of the wife, this book focuses on the labor of marriage, the breaking, and the freedom of finding a new way to live. There are, of course, same-sex marriages, and marriages with one or more nonbi-

nary or trans spouses. These relationships, like all relationships, are impacted by patriarchy and cultural biases, and
deserve to be scrutinized and studied as well. But the project
of this book is to examine the failure of the institution of
heterosexual marriage—the institution that pastors laud from
the pulpit, and politicians declare will save our country and
our children. Those marriages that romantic comedies por-
tray with soft-filtered lenses. Those marriages that still, at
the time of this book's writing, make up the majority of marriages in this culture.

I hope this changes. Sexuality is a spectrum, and so are
our relationships. And the more we can open the narrative
and allow for nuance the better our relationships and lives
will be. But the sacred cow I'm slaughtering for steak and
eating with a nice red wine is that of heterosexual marriages.
And I am doing it from the perspective of the partner who is
always asked to carry more than their fair share. The partner
who is paid less, provides more childcare, breaks more often,
and benefits less from marriage: the wife.

Women are taught that life is hard and then you die. It's
your strength and endurance in those hard times that makes
you a good person. Religion teaches us this. Capitalism
teaches us this. At wedding showers, older women will sit
around and laugh with younger women about the endless
cycles of socks on the floor, of unwashed dishes in the sink,
of anniversaries forgotten, words said in fury; they tell these
stories to say, This will be your life. This is marriage. This is
what it looks like. You will be miserable. But you cannot
leave.

I am one woman, and my life fell apart. But I'm also one

of many women who break every day. The divorce rate in America currently hovers near 40 percent, down significantly from its peak in 1979. And fewer and fewer Americans are choosing to marry. Dinah Hannaford, associate professor of anthropology at the University of Houston, spent years studying why women, specifically, are choosing not to marry. In her anthology *Opting Out: Women Messing with Marriage Around the Globe,* Hannaford and her colleagues posit that women aren't marrying simply because marriage holds them back from independence and opportunity, and they are finding fulfilling living situations with their friends and family. "Marriage has mostly not been a great situation for women historically and across the world, and they're trying to find alternative solutions," Hannaford said. "As new opportunities open up for women to be full people without it, they're opting for that." While popular culture—books, movies, and television shows—offer advice and show women marrying for love, women themselves seem to be running in the opposite direction. And so often, once they do marry, they eventually find they don't want to be married anymore.

Divorce is both personal and political. Our governments sponsor and prop up the institution of marriage with tax breaks and incentives, while making it nearly impossible to be a single parent. Nevertheless, millions and millions of people—mostly women—are looking up and realizing that they just cannot do this for one more minute: the gendered expectations, the unequal share of domestic labor, the exhaustion, everything. In droves, women are hitting the same wall I hit in my own eleven-year marriage so many years ago.

And we are prepared to endure the shame and self-criticism, the judgment of others, the painful separations, the clunky custody, and the loss of stability and income, if only to be free.

Of course, not all women want to get divorced. They love their husbands. They simply want the scale to slide just a little in their favor. They want Hawaii but will settle for Florida. This book is for them, too. To convince them to ask for everything they want and more, to raise the bar, and to show them if it breaks, there is a better life.

Do you want to know how I finally got my husband to do his fair share? Court-ordered fifty-fifty custody, that's how. And as readers will learn in this book, the same general principle applies to most areas of our liberation. True freedom and power begin with refusal.

For so long, women have been told that our relationships fail because of our weakness. When we give up, when we don't perform, when we can't handle it all, we feel inadequate. There is a million-dollar self-help industry dedicated to helping women cobble together the broken pieces of their marriage. As if it's our fault, as if the system of marriage wasn't built to break us from the beginning. As if it wasn't created to erase us and our ambitions and our hopes.

I want to tell you that breaking is our power. I want to tell you that walking away is a strength. I want to tell you that there is power in giving up. Yes, it's hard, and sure, you might cry putting together Ikea furniture at two A.M.—but there are other ways to build your life. Happiness is found through many different paths, and you do not have to waste years of your life hoping that maybe, one day, you'll finally get there. Maybe one day it will be your turn. You can be happy now. It's your turn now.

This is a book about the power of divorce, which means it's a book about the mechanisms of patriarchy, justice, love, and gender equality. Marriage, like any other cultural institution, is due for a reckoning. It is a state-sponsored endeavor, whose failure we shunt onto the individual. But its failure truly rests in the way inequality is built into our cultural systems. It's about how women's oppression now occurs largely through cultural norms and biases around domestic roles rather than the overt legal oppression our mothers and grandmothers grew up around. Although the legal oppression is making a comeback. It's also about how to foment a political and cultural revolution in your own life. It's about how specifically breaking the bonds of marriage, the system that was designed to oppress you, will open up your life to create something new and something better.

I believe that divorcées have a lot to teach everyone else about what goes into changing these norms. But I'm not arguing that you personally should get a divorce. I mean, not necessarily.

Our culture views divorce as a failure. One that requires a personal solution rather than a cultural one. Most divorce books focus on personal healing and self-help to get the divorcée back to dating and remarriage. But what if it's the whole system that is broken? Can you self-help your way through fundamental inequality? Can you meditate and manifest your way out of a culture and a politics that is continuing to strip you of your rights?

So often, in response to news of divorce, people reply with an "I'm sorry." But I think we should say "Congratulations." Congratulations for prioritizing yourself. Congratulations for being brave. Congratulations for the self-knowledge to know when to leave. "Self-knowledge," as Simone de Beauvoir wrote, "is no guarantee of happiness, but it is on the side of happiness and can supply the courage to fight for it." This book is not gentle divorce apologetics but a full-throated argument in favor of it—and the freedom that comes from having the courage to fight for your life rather than lose yourself in it.

———————

Cynthia tracked her husband down to a motel outside of Urbana. Not a hotel, a motel, off the highway. Here he was, a grown man, with a job, meeting a woman at a motel two hours away, the kind of place where all the rooms face the parking lot. They'd been married only eighteen months.

When Cynthia got to the motel, she asked the clerk at the front desk if her husband was there. He said he couldn't confirm the name—privacy issues, you know. But she wasn't leaving. Plus, she knew. His phone was pinging at this location. So, the clerk finally told her that the only guests they had that night were a man and a woman. Cynthia waited in the parking lot for hours. When she saw them come out of the room, she punched her husband right in the face.

"It was great," she tells me and a group of women as we drink wine at her house. "It's the kind of catharsis you only get in movies."

———————

2

Just a Girl in a Country Song

In high school, my older sister drove a 1972 Pontiac Catalina. The interior was teal with wide bench seats. My father bought it for her. He'd seen it in a driveway with a FOR SALE sign and thought it looked like it would keep her safe. It was 1998 and we lived in Vermillion, South Dakota. Some kids drove tractors to high school. It didn't matter what the car looked like because it was a way to transport ourselves away from the house that was falling down around us.

My parents moved from Texas to South Dakota in 1995. It was the height of the dot-com boom, and my dad got a job working for Gateway computers. Instead of living in Sioux City, like many executives, my parents moved us an hour away to Vermillion, a picturesque university town, where streets were lined with ramshackle Victorian homes and empty Bud Light cans.

My parents bought one of those Victorian houses, a former frat house. People in the neighborhood called it "the goat shit house," because of a rumor that fraternity brothers had smeared goat shit on the walls. The rumor was not confirmed, but it didn't have to be.

Immediately after we moved in, my mother began pulling down the kitchen walls. She enlisted the help of my brother and me, and together we pounded plaster and ripped lathes out of the wall. My mom hung plastic between the kitchen and the rest of the house, but it did little to protect the living areas from the construction zone. Plaster dust settled in a thin veil all over the house.

The three years we lived there, the house was in a constant state of destruction. Bats disturbed from the attic flew haphazardly through the house during the day. My dad would swing at them with a tennis racket, while my sisters and I screamed and covered our heads. A contractor showed up intermittently to use a Sawzall to cut more inexplicable holes.

The town was small, and we could walk or ride our bikes almost anywhere. But we were never truly free until my sister got her Catalina. The soundtrack to our freedom was the country music of the nineties. We'd listen to Deana Carter sing about summer love, and I'd look out the window to the flashing green and brown of the soy fields and imagine all the love I'd find when I could finally leave for good. There would be romance and adventure, and it would be just like strawberry wine.

I'd lean out the window and sing along with Alan Jackson about my little-bitty life and living on love. But more often it was Lorrie Morgan asking men what part of no did they not understand. Or Chely Wright singing about heartbreak and how we needed to just shut up and drive.

We'd been raised on country music. When we weren't listening to it or Christian pop or gospel, we were listening to Pete Seeger, James Taylor, Joni Mitchell, and Carole King. My mom played the guitar and the dulcimer and had a degree in music, and she'd tell us about the Scottish folk songs and African spirituals that made country music so uniquely American. Our mom orchestrated Christmas concerts for our small churches with twangy mountain songs. At home, she'd pull out her guitar and teach us "Old Joe Clark" and "The Rattlin' Bog."

I lived for those moments when we'd sing together as a family, our voices soft, mingling, making something that felt like magic. If my mother had her way, we would have turned into the Trapp family singers. My sister Jessie played the flute. Zach, who was just sixteen months younger than me, sang in a children's choir and could play songs by ear on the piano. My younger sisters could either hold a tune or were young and cute enough to get away with singing off-key. But no one was interested in my mom's plan for the family band, except for me, the least talented. I sang so loudly and so badly and with such enthusiasm, I was often asked to sing softer when we'd all line up on the church stage to sing "The Old Rugged Cross."

We weren't allowed to listen to other secular music, even though we did, hiding in the closet, around my sister's clock radio, or taping Alanis Morissette songs off the Top 40 countdown. But country was deemed safe, along with Christian contemporary. On its surface, country music reinforced tradition rather than upended it. It wasn't Madonna with her overt sexuality and embrace of queer culture. There was no riot grrrl writing "SLUT" on her stomach or singing about girl power. It was, at the time, primarily a white genre of music. There was no Salt-N-Pepa, no Whitney Houston, no Michael Jackson. Consequently, country was still safe for white Americans clinging to the past.

But it was still the nineties, and the women who were singing country songs were angry. Jo Dee Messina told them "bye bye" and Deana Carter looked at her man and sang, "Did I shave my legs for this?" Mindy McCready pointed out the hypocrisy of gender relations in America when she sang about coming home late, drinking beers, washing her truck, and watching ball games, and what? You got a problem with that? Well, guys do it all the time.

Women in country music had always been a little subversive; their boots had been made for walking after all.

These women were in love and angry and disappointed. They were not rejecting men outright. They were fighting with them, leaving them, coming back, then leaving them again. But isn't that what women always did? They weren't pushing for social change, just for Earl to change. They never wanted to burn down the system, the system had already been burned down—they just wanted their husband to come home for dinner on time and maybe mow the goddamn lawn. They didn't have a beef with the system; they had a beef with a few bad men. And in the nineties it seemed possible to ignore the rest. Girl power was en vogue. Girl rock. Women rappers. They were all singing their power anthems about sex and the system. Other women of nineties music, especially in punk rock and indie folk, saw the system as bad, and sang about it. But country music represented a way to express feelings of frustration without burning down the whole enterprise. Just pick off a few bad men with some poisoned black-eyed peas.

Dressed-up pain in sparkles and lipstick is what women in country music are good at; their looks and performance following standard cultural expectations for beautiful white women. But there never was going to be a sparkle bright enough, a smile wide enough, a skirt short enough, for women to be equal.

The lesson of country music was that no matter how we tried to make ourselves look pretty, no matter how we kowtowed to and believed in men, the system was designed against us. In 1995, we cheered as Hillary Clinton declared "Women's rights are human rights." We'd reached equality, hadn't we? I mean mostly, anyway. There was, of course, that problem with the pay gap, but women could do everything now. Even Betty Friedan, in her introduction to the twentieth anniversary edition of *The Feminine Mystique,* had declared that the problem now was not women's liberation but men's frustration. Everything was possible, we believed. Women could be everything a man could be.

But by the beginning of the 2000s, when thousands of people were burning the Chicks' CDs, we saw limits in the flames and the rage on the faces of those men. It was a lesson we would learn over and over.

x x x

In the middle of the twentieth century, a lot of female anger was channeled through the voices of men in country music, who played that anger as woman versus woman. "Pistol Packin' Mama" by Al Dexter was a 1940s hit about a woman going after her husband's lover. Wives in songs often went after the other woman, when it was the man they should have attacked. But in 1952, something changed. Hank Thompson's song "The Wild Side of Life" is a tale about a man who falls in love with a "honky tonk angel"—a woman who seduces a man and then leaves him for a life of freedom and barhopping. "I might have known you'd never make a wife," Thompson's plaintive, love-torn voice describes a liberated, oversexed floozy who just wants to drink and hang out with men, while he, a faithful man, mourns her faithlessness. He's lamenting that this woman doesn't want him—that a woman would choose a life of barhopping over a lifetime with him. Thompson's song wasn't different from many of the other country songs at the time. But the response to it was.

The American women of 1952 were the women Betty Friedan would write about a decade later: polished, thin-waisted, professional wives and mothers, forced back into the home after the brief liberation of WWII and the jobs the war machine had provided. They weren't oversexed; they were undersexed, educated, and overworked, cleaning and cooking and raising children for men who never seemed to come home. And they weren't happy about it. In the 1940s, divorce rates were higher than America had ever seen, at over 40 percent. And now, here was this man blaming them for their husbands not coming home.

Kitty Wells, a country singer with a then-flagging career, shot back. Her song "It Wasn't God Who Made Honky Tonk Angels," written by songwriter and musician J. D. "Jay" Miller, was a direct response to Thompson's scapegoating. Wells was initially reluctant to sing it, because it was a direct attack on a popular male artist, after all. But she had nothing to lose, and she recorded it. The song turns right around and blames men for the problems in the home: "Too many times married men think they're still single," proclaims Wells's reedy voice.

The song hit a nerve. It offended men and was banned by the Grand Ole Opry and NBC's radio network. But that didn't matter. The single quickly outsold Thompson's and pushed Wells to the top of the country charts. "It Wasn't God . . ." was the first number one *Billboard* hit for a solo woman artist on the country music charts.

The song's message, pushing back against the narrative and that sense of personal female rage, would reverberate through country music. Thirteen years later, Jeannie C. Riley would sing about the hypocrites at the Harper Valley PTA judging a single mom for her miniskirts. And twenty years later, Loretta Lynn would sing about "The Pill." Following Wells's example, as the second wave of the feminist revolution seeped into homes across America, the tired women of country music turned their rage away from the other woman and toward the man, as in Wanda Jackson's 1969 hit "My Big Iron Skillet."

These women opened up a vein of anger that flooded in

the 1990s: SHeDAISY, the Chicks, and Deana Carter would sing about their frustration with the roles of wife and mother and girlfriend. But the women of 1990s country still found themselves coming back to those frustrating beer-guzzling cowboys. Like Shania Twain in "Any Man of Mine," they'd demand better of a man, but a man still would be around.

Country music journalist and historian Marissa R. Moss explained to me in an interview that songs like these represented a personal rebellion, not a political one, which is why they were allowed on the airwaves. And even then, only tentatively so. Women artists still weren't played equally with male artists. "It was a delicate balance," Moss said. "Venting a personal frustration without upending the system." She pointed to Deana Carter's "Did I Shave My Legs for This?"

"She's complaining," Moss notes, "but she's not leaving, is she?"

But I do wonder how many of those songs were written to appease the listeners, the studio executives, and radio disc jockeys. The logic being: It's okay to kill Earl if the next song is about finding true love. Which song is the real one? Which song is the fiction? Or maybe it's all true. It's a push and pull that mirrors the struggles of so many women who long for freedom and equality, but also desire relationship and romance. Can't have a male partner without the patriarchy. So we suck it up. Shave our legs. Put on some jorts and jump in the truck. And wish that our friends in low places would learn how to go down on us. For years, I'd remind myself that even though I was unhappy, my ex was a good man and there wasn't much better out there. It would take me years to realize that the better thing I wanted did exist, and it was me.

But the Chicks, known then as the Dixie Chicks, would threaten that delicate push and pull between frustration and appeasement, simply because they were a success. "There was always going to be a backlash to the women of 1990s country music," Moss told me. "And songs like 'Ready to Run' and 'Goodbye Earl' were more directly rejecting of men than many others." When the Chicks criticized sitting president George W. Bush at a 2003 concert during the Iraq War, they not only ignited political frustrations but also exceeded the limits of what women in country music were allowed to do. They'd been tolerated when they were murdering an abusive husband but criticizing the president—that symbol of American male power—during a time of war, well, that had to be punished.

In 2003, advancements in gender equality were just a few years away from stalling out. In 2000, the number of women in the workforce had peaked at 60 percent participation. But the number of women going to college and graduating was on the rise. The gender gap in wages, which had stagnated in the eighties, was on its way up again. It's not that America was particularly progressive; it was just that the dot-com boom and the ubiquity of computers meant more jobs and more flexible workplaces, which made it easier for women to find employment. All of this progress would end just a few years later when the Great Recession of 2008 hit. Economic downturns always hit women and people of color the hardest. And we haven't made up for that lost time. During the COVID pandemic progress once again stagnated.

It's depressing to look at those charts, to see the numbers on women's progress going up and up, only to fizzle out.

America, once a leader in gender equality, now ranks forty-first among developed countries for equal pay. The backlash to the Chicks felt so acute and personal. It was the first time my generation would smash our heads into the glass ceiling. It wouldn't be the last.

The anger the Chicks incited erupted from a nasty part of American culture that needed to keep women in their place. It's a part of culture I'd see again in the 2016 election when men yelled at me online for voting with my vagina for Hillary Clinton, and in the spitting rage of the "Lock her up" chants. The election proved America would rather be led by Donald Trump than a competent woman. It's a rage I'd see again in the caucuses of 2020, when Americans said they wanted a woman for president, but not that woman, or that one, or the other one. We failed to nominate any of the female candidates that ran during the primary cycle that year. It was a message made clear: Capable, talented women would constantly be found lacking and wanting. And millennial women raised on the girl-power messages of the nineties would smash our heads again and again on the glass ceiling we were told has already been broken. But all of that would come later. In hindsight, 2003 was an omen of the toxic mix of jingoism and patriarchy that was to come. The lesson in people burning the Chicks' albums in the streets was that women were allowed to succeed only within the narrow confines of patriarchy. Fall afoul of that and burn.

Riding in that car with my sister, listening to the women of country, everything felt possible. She'd drive us to school, to doctor appointments or my tae kwon do class. Sometimes to friends' houses. And we'd take detours, driving out of town to just drive and we'd turn up the music and sing about all the cruelties we had yet to cry over and all the women we'd be. Driving a country road in the Catalina with my sister, I believed that anything was possible and that we were beautiful and that all we had to do was go forward with the wind in our hair, with everything broken behind us, and we'd be golden like the world before us.

She was two years older and so beautiful. Everyone told me so. The two of us had always shared a room as number one and number two of eight children. In Texas, we had a room painted lavender with colorful hearts our mom stenciled along the wall near the ceiling, our beds side by side. And when we were little, in the dark, she'd ask me to tell her stories, and I would tell her a story about two girls falling into the gutter and discovering a whole beautiful world underground and all their adventures fighting alligators and fish and living alone together, until I could hear the steady rhythm of her breathing. And then I'd click on my reading lamp and read. She could always sleep; I never could. Sometimes, I'd lie awake and try to match my breath to hers. If I could, perhaps I would just fall asleep.

Our parents were deeply conservative then and had told us that we would not date, we would "court": a process that involved the boy in question asking our father for permission to take us on supervised dates. Jessie did not do that. She started sneaking out. She slipped right out the window and disappeared. She began dating a boy who wore a cowboy hat and listened to Travis Tritt, who bought her a teddy bear and made out with her in the basement. He had a truck and blared Alan Jackson's "Little Bitty" from the speakers. And it was everything we'd sung about in all those songs on all those roads.

We had huge screaming matches about her boyfriend. Maybe I was having a hard time understanding the dissonance between rules and freedom. Maybe I didn't understand rebellion. After all, I would be a good girl until my thirties, when I'd divorce and blow up my life. So maybe I was, as she'd scream at me, jealous, so jealous of her. Not jealous because someone wanted her, but jealous that she had the courage not just to sing about life and freedom and love, but to find it.

In her song "One's on the Way," Loretta Lynn sings about how all the girls in New York City are marching for women's lib, but in Topeka, the faucet is leaking, the wash needs a' hanging, one kid's crawling, one's bawling, and one's on the way. It's a catchy and wry song. Maybe society was changing, but not for all women. And while Jackie O was out dancing, Loretta was in Kansas, just trying to survive. It's frivolous to talk about liberating women when you can't afford the gas money to even drive yourself out of town.

The issues of progress seem so remote when you have babies and not enough money to keep them all in diapers. It's not easy to untangle the choices of your life from the forces of culture. It's not easy to understand if what you've chosen was your choice or the only choice you had available to you in a world designed to limit you. But who has time for those questions when you are so tired you want to cry, one child needs more milk, the other wants to play Candy Land again, your husband wants to remind you that you haven't had sex in three weeks, and you just want to do your work?

What country music understands is that at a practical level, it's good to talk about liberating women, but most of us can barely afford to free ourselves. The songs of these country women communicate a kind of empowerment that reflects the complexities of our lives. So much of country music is a perfect embodiment of the struggle of marriage: a never-ending battle between the desire for freedom, the desire for more, and the men who seek you, haunt you, hunt you.

A tweet by Lucy Huber, an editor at the humor website McSweeney's, went viral in 2021. She wrote, "Why is male country music like 'hot girls in teeny tiny shorts I will make you my wife, bear my children, front porch, family values, casseroles' and female country music is like 'oops I killed my husband.'" It's not really a question. The answer is in the contrast. So glaring when put into a social media post. But it's easy to miss it when you live it.

I got engaged the year after America burned the Chicks' CDs. I was learning something I wouldn't fully comprehend for a long time. "For all the newly liberated women of the 1990s, the daughters of the second wave of feminism," Moss said, "the cancellation of the Chicks was an important lesson: The world is not limitless for a woman." Whatever equality we thought we had, whatever gains we thought we made, would go up in a pyre of Chicks CDs.

In a podcast, Dolly Parton would confess that the lesson of the Chicks would be one she took to heart, careful not to cross political boundaries that would prompt her fans to turn on her. Even the most powerful woman in country music was aware of the limits.

And that's what we couldn't see, my sister and me—two girls who'd never kissed anyone and had pledged our purity to Jesus and our daddy, driving down those roads. The roads would end. There would be limits.

But how could we know that then? What girls we were. How the world seemed so open and wide. How our hands snaked through the hot highway air. We knew the words to every song and weren't afraid to sing them. Innocence is a myth. Men had already hurt us. Our father's long unexplained absences, the fights between him and our mom. We'd been regularly hit by our father with a spanking spoon for talking back and fighting. Jessie was hit so hard, my father broke the bowl of the wooden spoon on her. My sister and I were already hurtling toward heartbreak. But in that Catalina, we felt like we were just waiting to be protagonists in the great love story of our lives.

My senior year of high school, my sister got married. And her marriage was a country song. But not the fun kind. There were fights and making up. There was always a return. We fought, too. I told her I hated her husband. Told her I thought he was cruel. I told her I thought he was misogynistic and a sexist. I wasn't wrong. But being right rarely makes people like you. I thought love would be our freedom. We'd hoped for wide open spaces, but she'd ended up trapped in a basement-level apartment that smelled of Axe body spray and cheap candles. And he couldn't pay the bills to keep the lights on.

But I guess I didn't end up much better. My bills were paid, but it was still a trap.

In 2015, my sister finally left her marriage. And two years later, in 2017, I would end my own. The year of my divorce, I started going on long drives just to cry. I didn't want to be alone in my house. I wanted to go somewhere, anywhere, but I was so broke. So I would get a large Diet Dr Pepper from a gas station soda machine (the one with the good ice) and drive and drive and listen to music and cry. I listened to Kesha and P!nk. But, mostly, I turned on the ladies of nineties country music. I listened to Trisha Yearwood and Martina McBride, Faith Hill, Terri Clark, and, of course, the Chicks.

The Chicks' *Fly*, the music that promised my sister and me our freedom, became the soundtrack to my heartache. Listening to the album nearly twenty years later, I felt like a failure. Why hadn't we run? Why hadn't we murdered our Earls? Why hadn't we stuck together?

The heterosexual narrative of country music celebrates love, our cowboys taking us away, claiming there is freedom in love. But it also carries a warning. Mary Anne and Wanda may kill Earl, but the very next song on the album opens with Natalie Maines's twang saying, "Hello, Mr. Heartache, I've been expecting you." I sang all those songs and felt all those contradictions as I reached my hand into the golden Midwestern air and looked for my freedom again.

Maryanne invited me into her home and showed me all the women she'd made. Hundreds of tiny paper women, trapped in bottles, climbing clocks. They were joyful and they were sad. They carried large flowers and rolled dice. Some of these paper women climbed ladders out of their jars, some were pasted on pieces of wood. Some simply sat alone on shelves. Her desk was covered with the discarded paper women.

As I looked at each woman, Maryanne told me the story of her divorce. She spent so many years supporting her husband and his art. He was an important artist. She raised their two girls.

And then, on the day their youngest daughter graduated, she overheard him on the phone with someone. She knew, she just knew. He'd been having an affair.

That night, after the party, she confronted him and he confessed. It was her friend, the wife of his friend. They'd been seeing each other for years.

She kicked him out. She kept the house. And she began making the army of paper women that were scattered throughout her studio. She invited me because she wanted me to see the women. Really see them.

By the time her story ended, we were sitting with glasses of wine, looking out the window through which she'd observed the world for the entirety of her marriage. We were watching the storm clouds part and reveal a pink sky. All the leaves on the trees were glimmering with the wet heat.

I understood why she put those paper women inside glass jars.

3

Down the Aisle

got married on July 25, 2005. It was a small wedding, with just ninety guests. The ceremony was held in the rose gardens on the campus of my picturesque Midwestern Lutheran college. I'd spent the previous two summers working on campus for the catering service, helping with the camps and conferences that came through while the students were away—hauling chairs, serving coffee and pastry to the Lutheran women's societies, checking in middle school campers, and getting yelled at by their suburban parents when I said, "No, they can't have fridges in the rooms." I liked the job, but I loved the campus. It was the first place I had felt free.

Margie, the head of campus catering, gave me a discount on food for the wedding, and I saved money by having pie instead of cake. I ordered flowers from Sam's Club with my parents' membership card and arranged them myself the night before with my friend Kristin. Pink roses and big white hydrangeas spilling out of mason jars on top of crisp white tablecloths.

The wedding was held midday with lawn games among the roses and a light lunch under the sweeping white canopy of a tent. Toasts were made with sparkling apple juice and lemonade. No wine, per my husband's request, plus I couldn't afford it. My sisters wore hats, and tulle fluttered in the July breeze. It was hot, but a thunderstorm, which had just missed the campus, poured on the neighboring town, cooling everything off just in time. My freshman-year roommate sang James Taylor's "How Sweet It Is (To Be Loved by You)" as the recessional.

It was a beautiful wedding; everybody said so. And it had cost me everything.

At the beginning of the school year, my younger sister Cathy had told the family she'd been sexually assaulted by another family member. The revelation tore my family apart. I was barely speaking to my older sister or my parents, who were trying to hold the family together, insisting that I forgive and move on. The man accused had denied everything, and I refused to invite him to the wedding. After initially filing charges, my parents decided not to pursue sending him to jail. And my sister was too young to press charges on her own. And so, when I was falling in love with the man I would marry, my sister was being hurt by another man. That year, while my family crumbled, I accepted an offer of marriage. I was clinging to what felt stable in a time when nothing felt stable.

I was so lonely. My best friends, Kate and Anna, had

graduated the year before. I was isolated from my college friends because my fiancé thought they were a bad influence: Too much drinking, he said. And I kept my distance willingly, because if people got too close, I'd have to tell them the truth about my family and my life. I was determined to be the good girl—I was Phi Beta Kappa, an RA, with a ring on my finger. And I was holding on so tightly to what I had been told was good and right, I could barely breathe.

I'd have long, tearful conversations with my mother and then sit down to read message boards on wedding planning websites. I'd scream into my pillow, then address save the dates. I'd have dreams that my family was in a house, each of us locked in a room alone, while the man who hurt my sister walked from room to room, stabbing us. And then I'd wake up, go to class, and call the catering company about pricing for white folding chairs. One night, as I lay crying in my room, I heard a rustling noise in the trash can. It was a bat. I immediately grabbed my large copy of *Maus* and put it over the lid then ran the trash can outside. I dumped the contents of the trash can on the lawn and screamed for the bat to fly away. "Be free!" I yelled. "Just go! Be free!" I started crying so hard I couldn't breathe. Eventually, security came by and helped me clean everything up. They thought I was drunk. I couldn't tell them the truth, that I was falling apart. Later, I told the story to my fiancé and his family as a joke, rather than the mental breakdown that it was.

I truly believed that if I could do everything correctly, get good grades, marry a good man, that I could fix this. So, every rose, every swath of tulle, every glass jar, every white fan carefully decorated with pink flowers, everything was a detail piecing together the reality that I wanted to exist. I would make this life good. And it would start with the perfect wedding.

That was the story of my life I wanted: the one where I had it all. I wanted that moment, the white dress, the cake, the voluptuous hydrangeas and velvet pink roses. I wanted someone waiting for me at the end of that aisle, full of love and hope.

Of course, I thought I could fix my life with a fairy-tale wedding. Because it's the remedy for every problem in our society. Politicians and columnists and policymakers all tell us that everything from childcare, income inequality, and healthcare to poverty, delinquency, and unwanted pregnancy can be solved with marriage. And the brokenness of marriage is a lucrative industry. There is a whole industry of books, television shows, movies, apps, websites, matchmakers, and advice givers dedicated to helping men and women (but mostly women) find marriage. The manic industry of heterosexual monogamous marriage is also propped up by governments, which provide tax breaks and financial incentives to married couples. Very few people will look at a couple and ask out loud why they got married. But they will ask every single person why they aren't married yet. An unmarried person is an unnerving presence. Heterosexual marriage is a metonymy for social order.

What pushed me down the aisle on July 25, 2005, was love, a desire for order, and the entire history of Western civilization.

The origins of marriage in the Western world begin with the Bible. "It is not good for man to be alone," the Lord God declares after the creation of Adam. From Adam's rib, God made Eve, Adam's partner. From man, God creates man's partner, woman. And gives the edict that a man should leave his family and marry his wife.

This is the root mythology of marriage: one man and one woman. Repeated ad nauseam in churches across the world. And yet, that's not how the early patriarchs practiced marriage. Marriage for Abraham, Isaac, and Moses was all about reproduction and resources. These patriarchs had multiple wives and concubines. The reality is that the so-called biblical model of marriage all too often involved one man, one woman, her servant, her sister, a concubine or two, and sometimes the Holy Spirit, when it comes time to knock up a virgin.

Raising human children is extraordinarily difficult, and early societies formed large family units for precisely this task. It required a lot of work and intragenerational and community support. Abraham and Sarah were not living in a suburban home with a piece of reproduced barn wood painted with the maxim "Live, laugh, love" on the walls. The early biblical patriarchs had multiple wives and large complex family units.

Before societies understood the concept of sperm and egg working together to make a child, many organized themselves around female deities and matriarchal rule. In ancient Libya, where women served in the armies and in government positions, children were raised by a community of men. The Mosuo of Yunnan in southwest China do not have a tradition of marriage. Children are raised in the maternal home, with no shared economic obligations with the fathers, who are largely absent from the task of child-rearing and living in their own maternal homes.

The exceptions aside, most societies have some form of marriage—some way of unifying relationships for the raising of children, and controlling the issues of inheritance, property, and paternity. But the variations in how marriages are formed and how they evolved are wildly divergent. The modern American marriage of a couple as a small world unto themselves, relying solely on each other for emotional and financial support, is a recent development in modern history. Because how could families have survived that way? They are barely surviving today. Popular mythology and preachers like to state that half of marriages in America end in divorce. This isn't exactly true. Divorce rates are hard to calculate. There is the "crude rate," which is the number of divorces among all people in a year. There is the "refined rate," which is the number of divorces among women in a year (researchers use women because their data reporting is seen as more reliable). Divorce rates can also be calculated by dividing the number of marriages in a year by the number of divorces. Also, many states have incomplete or unreliable data reporting. So, it's easy to read divorce numbers to be either shocking or hopeful, depending on your ideological agenda. In 2014, Claire Cain Miller writing in *The New York Times* declared that the divorce surge was over and one-third of all marriages would end in divorce. Some researchers contradicted her, stating that the divorce rate was rising. The back-

and-forth illustrates the complexities of the numbers and tracking the data. For example, how do you calculate marriages where couples separate but never divorce? Some numbers I found put the divorce rate around 40 to 45 percent, which is low. This is due in part to an increasing number of adults who are avoiding marriage altogether. But even if we go with the low 40 percent number for the likelihood that a marriage will fail, if 40 percent of Honda CR-Vs had engine failures, Honda would issue a recall.

For most of Western history, until feminist movements of the twentieth century worked to change laws of inheritance and property, marriages were contract deals designed to unite wealth and kingdoms, and form alliances. Fathers would give dowries to the husband's family, paying them to take his daughter away. Sons were means of protecting and accumulating property, while daughters meant the loss of property. According to a Yale University compilation of marriage and family customs collected in a database to synthesize centuries of cultural knowledge, "About 75 percent of societies known to anthropology involve at least one explicit and substantial transaction related to marriage, and most societies have more than one transaction." Your marriage is no exception; what do you think a ring is?

Anthropologists speculate that the custom of marriage was so widespread because it was a way to control paternity through the regulation of female sexual behavior. But even though marriage is nearly universal, the way it is practiced is not. The Guarani of South America practice trial marriage, where a man brings a woman into his home and together they act married. The woman cooks for the man's mother, and if everything works out, they're married. The equivalent to the practice of living together before marriage. Even today, more than 50 percent of the world's marriages are arranged. Marriage by choice is a modern invention.

Early biblical wives, according to the Torah, were not only supposed to be faithful, beautiful producers of male heirs, they were also supposed to provide economically for the household. "A wife of noble character, who can find?" the tenth verse in the thirty-first chapter of Proverbs begins. The chapter then lists the qualities of a godly woman who sews, cooks, cleans, and day trades, and looks hot doing it. These words are not some lost ancient text; they hang cross-stitched on the walls of my parents' home. And when I was married, they would be quoted in sermons and repeated in Bible studies.

Ancient Greek and Roman societies were no less unequal than the ones described in the Bible. Marriage was a property arrangement, a way to ensure the lines of paternity and citizenship. Love sometimes entered into the equation, but more often, love had nothing to do with who married whom. Men in ancient Greece were allowed to seek emotional and sexual validation outside of marriage, but women were not. A man with a lover was a man. A woman with a lover was a disgrace. Legally an abused wife could escape her husband only by returning to her father.

Roman law allowed marriage to occur with the consent of the bride, the groom, and the bride's father. The mother's consent was not legally necessary. Additionally, a bride and groom could enter a marriage of affection. This was a legal change marking a precedent for what would become the shift of marriage from reasons of property to reasons of the heart. But it's important to note that women were allowed to be married and promised in marriage at an early age with the emphasis on reproductive capabilities. Whatever else marriage was about, it was primarily about producing children.

The past is never far from us. Marriage is an institution built on the fundamental inequality of women. As much as we'd like to think everything has changed, you only have to attend a modern wedding in a church and see a bride dressed in virginal white, with a veil, see a couple exchange rings, a symbol of bondage, and know that no matter how transformed the institution is, it's still inherently unequal. A wedding is still woman's work—setting the stage for a partnership where she will still cook, clean, work, raise kids, and feel like she needs to look good doing it. And just because a couple doesn't quote scripture doesn't mean the model still doesn't hold its power.

Second only to the Bible in its influence on formulating our idea of Western marriage is William Blackstone's *Commentaries on the Laws of England,* published between 1765 and 1770. In his analysis, Blackstone codifies the spiritual union of the Bible—"two become one"—into the legal sense of a wife becoming subsumed under her husband, who now possesses all she possesses, and has the legal right to punish her. These laws are best summarized by Blackstone as "the old common law fiction that the husband and wife are one . . .

[and] the one is the husband." These laws of "coverture" have haunted women for centuries, well into the modern era, as second-wave feminists of the 1960s and '70s worked to remove laws prohibiting married women from opening bank accounts and applying for lines of credit. In her book *Looking for Love in the Legal Discourse of Marriage,* Renata Grossi writes, "The common law tradition teaches us that a marriage is a unity between two people, but the relationship between them is not equal." Women were given protections under the law, but, Grossi explains, they were the same protections offered to infants and lunatics.

What about women who were abused in their marriages? Did the laws of marriage help them? Given that 70 percent of divorces today are instigated by women, it's fair to speculate that women of the past weren't happier inside the social system of marriage.

The Catholic Church, ironically, has a lot of stories of women who would have rather died than marry. The legend of Saint Wilgefortis first appears in religious literature around 1400, and tells of a young princess whose father, the king of Portugal, arranged for her to be married. Wilgefortis had taken a vow of chastity and prayed that the Lord would make her repulsive to men. In answer to her prayers, she miraculously grows a beard. But her pagan father, in a rage, has her crucified. In religious icons she is symbolized as a bearded woman on a cross. She became the patron saint of abused and unhappy women desperately wishing to avoid marriage.

Some art historians theorize that the tale of the saint arose out of confusion over the image of the *Volto Santo di Lucca,* a carving of a crucifix that depicts Christ on the cross in a full-length tunic, and that Wilgefortis never existed. Whether true or not, the legend was powerful, gaining popularity in the fifteenth and sixteenth centuries and going by many different names, including Saint Uncumber. She was an early model of how to opt out of a system rigged against women. She offered a way to turn undesirability, ugliness, and queer identity into something powerful and saintly. It could be coincidence that the story of Wilgefortis arose around the same time the church began to take a primary role in regulating marriage, but I don't think it is. As long as there has been marriage, it has been about controlling the actions of women. And women have been finding ways to subvert its control.

Of course, many women did and still do find value in the social acceptability and relative stability of marriage. These ideas are manifest in the novels of Edith Wharton and Jane Austen and today on TikTok, where women will joke that they have wedding plans, but no fiancé. So much has changed, but so much hasn't. And in a society where women are still paid less than their male counterparts and earn even less when they begin having children, marriage, if you can get it, seems to offer a respite from all of that. In her campaign against the Equal Rights Amendment, Phyllis Schlafly successfully tapped into an undercurrent of fear in the culture that women could lose the status they procured through marriage. Women benefit from the protectorship of patriarchy, Schlafly argued.

What this logic conveniently forgets is that half of American women have experienced intimate partner violence.

And women are more likely to be murdered by their male partner than by anyone else. Protectorship sounds nice, but in reality it's a violent prison.

More than war, more than kingdoms rising and falling, it's the drama of love and marriage and the ensuing heartbreak that buttress the stories we tell ourselves. And literature provides a perfect mirror for cultural anxieties that surround what a marriage and a wife should be. Canonically, one of the first novels written is the story of a marriage. Samuel Richardson's 1740 novel *Pamela* is written as a series of letters from the perspective of Pamela Andrews, a virtuous servant. Pamela is pursued by her employer, Mr. B, who repeatedly assaults her and attempts to take her virginity. Pamela valiantly resists his advances until she's molested by him in bed, which sends her into hysterics. Eventually, Mr. B reads Pamela's letters, which show her side of the story. He apologizes and proposes, and she eventually accepts, explaining that she resisted him because she was afraid he'd take advantage of her and refuse to marry her. The marriage of Pamela and Mr. B takes place in the middle of the novel, and the rest of the book is devoted to Pamela's difficulty shifting from a servant to the wife of a landowner.

At one point after their marriage, Mr. B's sister Lady Davers comes to the home and accuses Pamela of being a sham and reveals Mr. B has a daughter by another servant. Eventually, Pamela wins over the judgmental Lady Davers, finds Mr. B's daughter, and brings her to live with them. The full title of the novel is *Pamela; or, Virtue Rewarded,* and details a woman under attack who holds on to her virginity at all costs and is rewarded for it. Pamela's desires and lusts beyond the preservation of her virtue are never explored. And her reward for her dedication to her virtue is a marriage to the man who was her attacker.

Over a century later, Tolstoy's *Anna Karenina* would chronicle the downfall of a woman who wants more than what her married life offered. She has an affair, and this act of transgression sends her into a spiral; she eventually steps in front of a train. Tolstoy, the moralist, is sending a message about where wanting will get you.

The wants of Lydia Bennet, the younger sister of Elizabeth Bennet in *Pride and Prejudice,* nearly lead her to social and moral ruin, when she runs away with the dashing and dastardly George Wickham. Her virtue is saved by Mr. Darcy, who uses his vast fortune to bribe Wickham to make an honest woman out of Lydia. Austen's novels of middle-class domesticity always show marriage as a highly sought-after institution that so often leads to misery. Happiness, Austen seems to indicate, is the exception rather than the rule.

Gustave Flaubert's *Madame Bovary* tells the story of the ruthless, selfish, vain, and tragic Emma Bovary and draws a portrait of a marriage, thwarted hope, and ruinous desire. Emma is dissatisfied with her life as the wife of a small-town doctor and begins a series of affairs. She also spends money on the sly and throws herself into debt. Emma's husband, Charles, is a simp for his wife. Flaubert is critical of his subjects, inviting the reader to judge everyone and everything. But there are moments of devastating compassion. When Emma is pregnant, she wishes for a boy, because "A man at least is free; he can explore every passion, every land, overcome obstacles, taste the most distant pleasures. But a woman is continually thwarted. Inert and pliant at the same time, she must struggle against both the softness of her flesh and subjection to the law. Her will, like the veil tied to her hat by a string, flutters with every breeze; there is always some desire luring her on, some convention holding her back." Emma has a daughter, and when Charles tells her the news, she faints.

We'd like to believe that modern women aren't so simpleminded. But I remember the birth of my own daughter so well. We hadn't learned her sex, and I had been prepared for a boy. After all, as my in-laws loved to remind me, they were a family of men. But she was born, blond and pink. "You have a girl," the doctor said, and I was immediately filled with terror for what the world held for her. Holding her those first sleepless weeks, I'd often cry, thinking of all that had been done to me, wishing a kinder world for her.

Caught in financial ruin, Emma eventually takes a lethal dose of arsenic. Her death, much like her life, is far more painful and messy than she anticipated. Charles dies after reading letters written by Emma to her lovers, and their daughter is forced to work in a cotton mill.

Women who desire more than the quiet domestic life are so often punished in the stories we tell. And women who do desire love and family often find it claustrophobic. The trope of the thwarted and trapped wife still finds an audience today. The 2021 novel *Nightbitch* by Rachel Yoder tells the story of a wife and mother so trapped by the demands of her domestic duties that she literally transforms into a dog at night. Novels like *The Nursery* and *The School for Good Mothers* depict being a wife and mother as dark dystopian states of being. It's no wonder then, that an increasing number of women are opting out of marriage and motherhood altogether.

The history of marriage is also the history of divorce. Divorce found its legal pathways because King Henry VIII couldn't sire a male heir. In 1522, the king fought with the Vatican to obtain a divorce to marry Anne Boleyn. Famously, this didn't work out for her. Spoiler: She was beheaded. And Henry VIII would divorce one more wife after that. But his divorces didn't open the floodgates to divorce in England. In fact, his bad example made England far more restrictive, and getting a divorce required an act of Parliament until 1857. In that year there were 324 divorces granted, and only three of them were instigated by women.

Americans may not have invented divorce, but we did make it great. Glenda Riley's book *Divorce: An American Tradition* posits that Americans have always led the world in divorce rates. In 1620, the Pilgrims made marriage a civil, rather than a religious, agreement. Records show that the Pilgrims granted at least nine divorces, and the first was granted in the Massachusetts Bay Colony. In 1639, the wife of James Luxford was granted a divorce because her husband already had a wife. In the 1830s, the Frenchman Michel Chevalier toured America and noted that divorce was easier to attain in the new country than it was in Europe.

Divorce fit well with American mythos of freedom, democracy, and individualism. If men escaping the law could come to America and find a new life, why not women? In 1771 or 1772, Thomas Jefferson, never one for being good at dating his notes, began writing a brief in defense of divorce on behalf of John Blair, who wanted to end his tumultuous nineteen-month marriage. The brief was never filed because John Blair died. But Jefferson's writing connects the freedom of divorce to the ideals of the Revolution. Under the title "Arguments pro," Jefferson wrote the following: "Cruel to continue by violence an union made at first by mutual love, but now dissolved by hatred. . . . Liberty of divorce prevents and cures domestic quarrels." It sounds liberating, but Jefferson was advocating for freedom for men and men only. The other notes in his documents show he believed that a wife was obligated to have sex with her husband and produce children. Freedom, for Jefferson, when it came to marriage and the founding of America, was freedom for white men.

Jamestown, founded as a puritanical theocracy, allowed a kind of marital separation, where the couple could live apart, the husband would support the wife, and neither could remarry. After the colonies declared independence, the southern states (except South Carolina) began to allow legislative divorces, where the couple could apply for the absolute dissolution of their marriage from the state's lawmakers. Overwhelmed by the number of divorce petitions, lawmakers eventually turned the process over to the courts. It's important to note that this freedom was for white people only. Black people were still largely enslaved. But they were often mentioned in divorce petitions, where husbands blamed their wives for bearing "mulatto" children, or wives accused their husbands of cruelty for bringing enslaved women into the marriage bed.

The reasons for many of these early divorces are no different from the reasons people today have for splitting up—abuse, intoxication, and adultery. Riley's analysis of the data concludes something that also parallels modern marriage: Most of the divorce petitions in the state of Virginia were sought by women. A lot of these women so desperately wanted to be free that they shared their private humiliations with an entire legislative body. I wonder about all the women without the means or stamina or support to seek divorces. What were their lives like? How much greater their humiliations?

On November 9, 1805, Robert Cartwright placed an ad in *The Tennessee Gazette and Mero-District Advertiser* for his runaway wife. "I do hereby forewarn all persons from crediting my wife Polly Cartwright, on my account, or harboring her, as she has left my bed and board without any just cause. I am therefore determined to pay no debts of her contracting, and will prosecute any person harboring her, with the utmost rigor of the Law." Ads for runaway wives that mostly absolved the husbands of their debts rather than calling for the wives' return filled the pages of early newspapers.

In the 1800s, the Midwestern states of Ohio, Indiana, Illinois, and Iowa gained reputations for quickie divorces. Ohio and Indiana eventually put restrictions on residency requirements, pushing people into Iowa and Illinois, and

eventually the Dakota Territory. In 1889, the U.S. Bureau of
Labor tallied 328,716 divorces between 1867 and 1886. And
most of the divorce seekers, two out of three, were women.

In her book *The Divorce Colony,* historian April White
tells the story of women who escaped to the Dakota Territory
to get a divorce. One woman, Blanche Molineux, took the
four-day train ride to Sioux Falls to establish residency in
order to divorce her husband Roland, who had been tried
for the murder of one of Blanche's friends. Although Roland
was ultimately acquitted, the trial rocked the nation, with
Blanche named as the center of a love triangle and blamed
for the murder. Sioux Falls at the time had become a divorce
colony, where women with the means could go to establish
their residencies and seek their divorces. They formed a
motley band of outlaws, an Ex-Wives Club on the frontier.

Blanche got her divorce. But her notoriety brought scrutiny to the divorce colony, and lawmakers extended the time
required to establish residency. Then, Nevada took up the
mantle as the quickie divorce capital of America. It's important to note that none of these quickie divorces were actually
that quick; they took months, and they were reserved for
those who had the means to make them happen.

Freedom was what so many American women wanted,
and they would do anything to get it. After all, America had
been founded on the promise of freedom. In April 1848,
forty-four married women in western New York wrote to the
New York state legislature citing America's founding document, the Declaration of Independence, noting, "Your Declaration of Independence declares, that governments derive
their just powers from the consent of the governed. And as

women have never consented to, been represented in, or recognized by this government, it is evident that in justice no allegiance can be claimed from them. . . . Our numerous and yearly petitions for this most desirable object having been disregarded, we now ask your august body, to abolish all laws which hold married women more accountable for their acts than infants, idiots, and lunatics."

That same year, American suffragists held the Seneca Falls Convention, where women argued not just that they should have the right to vote and hold property, but that marriage itself should be changed. Women, created equally, should be treated equally. And change began to happen. In 1848, New York passed a married women's property act. It wasn't the first—that had been passed in Mississippi, nearly a decade before. But after New York, other states followed—passing laws that allowed women to own property, keep income, and have a right to property acquired through marriage.

As women became more financially free, marriage became more about love and sex rather than commerce (or so we told ourselves). But it was a slow change. Women couldn't get a mortgage or own credit cards without the approval of a father or husband until 1974. For centuries, rape was defined as between a man and a woman "not his wife," establishing the fact that no matter the reality, legally, a husband could do what he wanted with his wife, and he did. Those laws began to change in the '70s but even now, some states like South Carolina treat marital and nonmarital rape differently.

x x x

The story of marriage is just as much about who is included in the narrative as it is about who is excluded. The book *Far More Terrible for Women* is a collection of the stories of women who were enslaved in America before the Civil War. These women recount love unions ripped apart because it was more advantageous for their owners to have them married to someone else, and partnerships made for breeding purposes, only to be ended when husbands were sold away or killed. One woman, Louisa Everett, who was ninety when she was interviewed, recalled that on the plantation where she lived, enslaved people were forced to have sex with one another. If the owner thought a certain couple would have good children, he'd force them to have sex even if they were married to other people. Everett was married to her first husband when the plantation owner, a man she called Mister Jim, called her and an enslaved man named Sam over to him and ordered Sam to take off his shirt. Then Mister Jim asked Everett if she could stand such a strong man. Mister Jim was carrying a bullwhip, so Everett said yes.

"Well," she recalled, "he told us we must get busy and do it in his presence, and we had to do it. After that, we were considered man and wife." Another woman, Julia Brown, recalled her aunt and uncle being married but living on two separate plantations; they were allowed to visit only on Wednesdays and Sundays. One Sunday her uncle went to visit his wife and she'd been sold. He never found her again.

Slavery in America was used to prop up white families with free labor, while tearing Black families apart. Later, government support for families, such as free childcare for working women during World War II and veterans housing, would be denied to Black families. Every cultural force in America was working to tear Black families apart, while shaming them for not being married. In *Veil and Vow*, her cultural history of Black marriages, sociologist Aneeka Ayanna Henderson writes, "Black women's unfreedom is made plain through the fictional depiction of domestic or intimate partner violence, rape, and sexual assault, and the state's violent interventions in their private lives. These interventions, from both political and cultural institutions, often rehearse neoliberal discourse, bolstering familiar order and privatized solutions as they reduce female subjectivity to marital status. They surreptitiously encourage African American women, imagined as the least desirable, to suffer through abuse and assault in order to sustain the facade of bourgeois nuclear family, made politically important for African American people."

It's hard to get married when the culture views you as less desirable. Henderson calls this "marriageocracy," a portmanteau of "marriage" and "meritocracy." The word suggests "that a free, unregulated, and equitable romance market animates marriage and the idea that it can be obtained with the cogent but misleading trinity of individual hard work, resilience, and moxie," Henderson explains. But this idea isn't borne out by reality. According to a recent Pew Research Center study, Black women are more likely to be single than any other demographic. A 2014 OkCupid survey of dating behavior from 2009 to 2014 found that Black women were viewed as the least desirable dating cohort. And if you should get married, it's hard to stay married when the state is more likely to incarcerate Black women and Black men, and social services are more likely to get involved in their children's lives. Additionally, interracial marriage was illegal in many states until the *Loving v. Virginia* Supreme Court decision of 1967. Author Michael Warner sums it up perfectly in his book *The Trouble with Normal,* when he calls marriage "nothing if not a program for the privileged."

Today, nearly half of all Black women have never been married. That's compared with 32 percent of all American women. Marriage, simply put, can't be a solution to societal ills, because it isn't accessible to all people in our society. For centuries, traditional marriage was illegal for gay people. It wasn't until 2015 that the Supreme Court recognized same-sex marriage as a constitutional right. In the Queer Manifesto, a defining document of the social and political movement ACT UP written in 1990, the author points out that for centuries, because of stigma, many queer people were consigned to expressing their feelings of love through art, therefore defining cultural conceptions of love while being denied the ability to access the legal institutions of love. The documentary *Invisible: Gay Women in Southern Music* highlights this point perfectly, telling the stories of lesbian country songwriters who cloaked their sexuality to remain in the industry, writing songs that defined and expressed and reinforced notions of heterosexual love.

Excluded from the institutions of heteronormative marriage, Black and queer people have found fuller ways of living. In the essay "Single Black Women and the Lies About Our Love Lives," the author Minda Honey notes,

The pandemic has only deepened my ambivalence about the supposed connection between matrimony and happiness. The surge in divorces these past few years made me question what these married women I'd often envied learned during the months they were shut-in with a spouse? Yes, the pandemic has been lonely for singles. But unlike many partnered women, I had not needed to drop out of the workforce to be the primary caregiver for children, nor had I found myself grumbling over being laden with an unfair portion of the household management. Often, when discussing singleness, there is a focus on what is lacking from a life unpartnered. Rarely do we consider what must be exchanged for a life lived with someone else.

Honey then goes on to describe the different ways Black women are redefining their relationships and their lives. Being forced out of the heterosexual marriage market has become a place of freedom rather than exclusion.

Whenever we tell the history of marriage, it's important to know who is excluded: the poor with no property to transfer, queer people, people who are too fat or too thin, the women used for sex then discarded because they weren't considered high class enough to be wives, the enslaved, the sluts, the single moms, women of color. These are the Liliths in the myth of marriage.

The story of Lilith is derived from the biblical story of Adam and Eve and the creation. Genesis recounts two versions of the creation, one where God makes man and women in his own image. The other is where he creates women from the rib of man. Mandaean and Jewish mythology tells the story with two women. Lilith, the first woman, who is Adam's equal and who rejects the Eden created by the Lord, is banished and becomes a demon. And Eve, made from man, the good woman—who still isn't good enough—who gets both Adam and herself tossed out of paradise. Other interpretations of the Bible reject the existence of Lilith altogether. But if Western ideas of heterosexual marriage are rooted in the Christian and Jewish tradition of the union of Adam and Eve, then the woman lingering on the shadows of that story, even if she is a ghost of mythology, becomes relevant.

I imagine her hovering just outside of Eden, smoking, waiting for the others to be cast out, too. And they always are. Because it doesn't matter how pretty you are or how good you are at roasting chicken or cleaning the house, you will fail. Your body will not produce an heir. You will commit that unforgivable female sin of getting old. You will become boring. You will nag about socks. You will eat of the forbidden fruit. Even now, the Liliths know that marriage remains a vehicle for the strict regulation of money, property, inheritance, sexuality, and female desirability. And anyone who falls afoul is tossed out of Eden.

Historian Randal Olson created a chart tracking American divorce rates over the course of 144 years. Beginning in 1867, the chart shows the number slowly rising with a dip in the 1930s due to the Great Depression and a leap in the number after WWII. The chart seems to show that when economic hardship hits America, the divorce rate drops or holds steady; after all, it's hard to spend money on lawyers when there isn't much money to go around and the economy is uncertain. Historians attribute the leap in divorces at the end of WWII to the ending of the hastily cobbled together war marriages. Both divorce and marriage rates would drop in the 1950s, as women who were free to work while the men fought the war were forced back into the home. This restriction of women, and their unhappiness over it, brought about the second wave of feminism of the 1960s and '70s, in which women fought for equal pay, the right to work, financial freedom, and no-fault divorce. These freedoms caused a wave of divorces, with divorce rates in America hitting 50 percent. Since then, the rate of divorces has leveled out, and as I write this book the divorce rate sits at 2.3 per 1,000 people for the year 2022. Divorce is not immune to the cultural and political forces of history, because marriage and divorce are an essential pillar of society.

As such, criticizing marriage and telling the truths about the emotional lives of married women have always been a fraught enterprise that kicks up backlash, obfuscating the reality. In 1987, researcher Shere Hite published *Women and Love,* the third installment in her groundbreaking research into the lives of 4,500 American men and women, and found that despite pushes for equality, four-fifths of American women felt their marriages were unequal; 84 percent of respondents were not satisfied with their relationships; and 95 percent reported "emotional and psychological harassment" from their husbands. Instead of causing a cultural reckoning, Hite and her research were attacked. Newspapers ran stories about her slapping a driver for calling her "dear" and the time she answered the phone and pretended to be her own assistant. Bizarre maybe, but understandable for a woman who found herself thrust into the spotlight of a culture and its press that wanted to discredit her work. Essentially, in response to the news that women thought their partners were defensive and difficult and not listening to them, American men did not listen.

Whenever I point out the inequality in marriage, a man inevitably will bemoan the loss of marriage in our culture. The "whatever happened to the good old days when people stayed married" flavor of cultural critique is baseless and boring. But it persists because, as Susan Faludi points out in her seminal work of cultural analysis, *Backlash*, the one constant of marriage is that men have benefited from the institution. Study after study, across the decades, shows that married men are more likely to be healthier and happier than their unmarried counterparts. Faludi quotes sociologist Jessie Bernard, who wrote in 1972, "There are few findings more consistent, less equivocal, and more convincing than the sometimes spectacular and always impressive superiority on almost every index—demographic, psychological, or social—of married, over never-married men. Despite all the jokes about marriage in which men indulge, all the complaints they lodge against it, it is one of the greatest boons of their sex." Meanwhile, women are far less likely to remarry after a divorce than men.

So what is marriage supposed to be in modern America? Stripped of commerce, political necessity, and divine mandate, modern marriage is supposed to be the union of souls.

A 2021 survey found that 60 percent of American adults believe in the concept of a soulmate. We tell ourselves that true love happens completely outside of the forces of culture and time. In *Serendipity*, Sara, played by Kate Beckinsale, meets Jonathan, played by John Cusack. They are both dating other people, so they decide to throw their chance at love to the fates. He writes his number on a five-dollar bill that he uses to buy gum. She writes her number in the book *Love in the Time of Cholera*, which she promises to sell. After years of not seeing each other, they by chance encounter the five-dollar bill and the book. As another character notes, "Life is not merely a series of meaningless accidents or coincidences, but rather, it's a tapestry of events that culminate in an exquisite, sublime plan." In each telling, modern marriage and, by extension, modern love, is an unknowable otherworldly force, rather than what it actually is—a product of race, class, and culture. Marriage was at least more honest when it involved a dowry.

More realistically, marriage in the United States still exists as a state-funded institution. In lieu of a social safety net, states hand out grants to marriage counseling and seminars. As of 2022, SNAP recipients in the state of Iowa receive a letter touting the benefits of a "healthy marriage." The woman who sent me the letter she received was a recent divorcée who told me by email that the letter made her feel like the government was calling her a failure, "[that if] I had been in a healthy marriage I wouldn't be on SNAP now, and that is obviously the goal. . . . The document doesn't talk about how to have a healthy marriage, so we know the goal isn't really education. . . . Just this little innocuous document letting all of us sad little welfare peasants know that we should be married." As if being miserable and staying off welfare were preferable to being happy and having a social safety net.

In 2022, the Republican Study Committee's (RSC) fiscal report "Blueprint to Save America" advocated moving SNAP benefits to a discretionary block grant program that would cut out federal rules and oversight and allow states to change work requirements. Throughout the document, the RSC repeatedly emphasizes that marriage and family should be the focus of these programs, pointing out that being a single parent (specifically a single mother) tends to lead to poverty. (A search of the document reveals that the term "single mother" appears four times, "marriage" appears twenty-six times, and "single father" appears zero times.) The solution? Force people into marriage in the name of cutting the social safety net.

It's not a new plan or even a secret one. It's not even just a Republican plan. State-funded marriage initiatives have been a policy priority under Bill Clinton, George W. Bush, and Barack Obama. And the logic of each of the programs has always been, as Senator Marco Rubio of Florida stated in 2014, that marriage is the "greatest tool to lift women and children out of poverty."

But maybe instead of discouraging divorce and forcing people into marriages for financial security, we should make a more equitable society. There is research evidence that suggests that countries with well-funded social safety nets have less divorce, fewer instances of child abuse, and less crime. A 2019 article on the Census Bureau website points out that in societies where divorce is relatively easy to access, "The number of marriages increases by at least 9%. Female suicides decrease by 8% to 16% and domestic violence decreases by around 30%. Women start working more outside of the home—up to 7 percentage points more—increasing their economic clout in a marriage by bringing income that they control into the home."

It is possible to have a happy and equal marriage inside an unequal system. But the system itself will always subsume the female partner. I had economic stability, a home, and children, but the cost had been my entire loss of self. And sure, perhaps your man—your single man—is worth the cost. A successful magazine editor once whispered to me at a bar that marriage was a scam. She was happy with her husband because she loved him, so it was still worth it. But some days she didn't know why. "Men are human and relationships are good, but marriage? It's a pyramid scheme." What she meant was that couples look happy, movies show us romance and marriage as the ideal, and that convinces other people to want that, too. We are afraid of dying alone, but no one really knows lonely better than a married woman sitting next to her silent husband.

At my bridal shower hosted by my mother, the women from her church laughed and joked about the horrible things their husbands did, from going out drinking till three A.M. after a new baby was born to letting laundry pile up on the floor for days. It felt like a bleak sort of reality. And their stories helped normalize my misery as a joke for too long.

In a TikTok that went viral in September 2022, getting more than 370,000 likes, a woman plays two characters—

a housewife from the 1950s and a woman in 2022. The woman from 2022 tells the housewife she's liberated now and can chug coffee in front of a computer all day while she works her liberated office job. "So," the '50s wife says incredulously, "I have to work full-time while still managing my house full-time?" The implication is that women were freer in the 1950s, when they had to appease only a husband rather than a husband and a boss. Better to be a ball and chain than a ball and chain and a cog in the wheel of capitalism.

I understand this. If women have to work for "the man," it might as well be for just one man, and a man who ostensibly loves her. But it's an upsetting logic, presuming that marriage is still the work of a woman, rather than a partnership of equals. Plus, that logic doesn't parse. All it does is economically isolate women. And a wife is far more likely to be abused by her husband than a stranger, and stay-at-home moms are more likely to be depressed and anxious. Women of the 1940s and '50s were very unhappy, and there was, in fact, an entire cultural revolution over it. Also, a woman who is economically free is free to choose a partner out of choice and not a necessity. Since I've become divorced and started making my own money, my entire relationship with relationships has changed. With economic freedom came my freedom to say no to men who offered me less than what I wanted. And the knowledge that without them, I'd be fine.

In *The Second Sex,* Simone de Beauvoir argued that marriage is premised on a man treating a woman as a person enslaved while making her feel like a queen. She also notes, "It is more comfortable to endure blind bondage than to work for one's liberation; the dead, too, are better suited to the earth than the living." Beauvoir's words feel like a face slap from the past, reminding modern women how long we've been struggling with the bondage of marriage. I know what she means; fighting to untangle a life from the expectations of marriage was far harder than getting married, and perhaps even harder than just giving up and staying married.

There is a picture of me from my wedding that I think about often. The wind had blown my veil over my face, and I am laughing trying to push it away. I remember that feeling, like my veil was the froth on a huge wave and I was being carried out to sea, pulled by forces I didn't understand. I look so young and happy, lost in a cloud of tulle.

There is so much in that picture that you don't see. How tired I was. How I'd developed an eye twitch from the stress of that year. How the night before I'd cried because my mother had called me selfish. And how desperately I wanted to leave that wedding. How I'd begged to elope. I wonder if someone had taken me aside and told me I didn't have to do this, would I have flown away? Or would I have married anyway?

The woman is an editor, *was* an editor. She laughs and corrects herself. I meet her at a party in Washington, D.C. She's tall and blond and holds a glass of white wine in her manicured hands. I tell her I'm working on a book about divorce, and her eyes narrow.

"I want one of those," she tells me in a whisper. "A divorce. I want to leave."

She's married to a very wealthy man, she tells me, and all she has to do is take care of the children and read books and go to parties with him looking beautiful.

"I think, actually, it would be a problem for him if I did try to do something more," she says. She thinks she should feel lucky, but she tells me she lives in a beautiful trap.

"Then you should go," I tell her.

Someone comes and whisks her away, and I don't talk to her again until the party is winding down. She finds me to say it was nice to meet me. "Forget what I said about my husband, I didn't mean it!" she tells me brightly.

I squeeze her hand, and I refuse to forget.

4

Why Should I Change My Name?

From the first day of my marriage, I became "the wife." This was a joke, my husband told me when I objected. *Just a joke.* His term of endearment for me. But for him I'd changed my last name and moved to a state where I had no job, no friends, and no family. Whoever I had been and whoever I wanted to be now seemed lost inside this new person who was called "the wife" and watched *Seinfeld* reruns while searching for a job. We hadn't lived together before we married. And when we moved, I was the one without a job. So this wife immediately began cooking and cleaning and doing the laundry.

The fight ended five years into our marriage when I gave birth and I became "Mom."

Who are we if we are not defined by our relationships? When we are born we become daughter, son, sister, brother, half-sibling, stepchild, grandchild, niece, nephew, Aquarius with a rising sign of Scorpio. We come into the world caught in a tangle of identity. Our mother looks at us and sees our father. Our father looks at us and sees his little sister. Our grandmother sees in us her own father. There are thousands of studies that look at what makes our identities and just as many conclusions—wealth, birth order, race, country, gender, and the dictates of DNA. More mystically there are astrological birth charts that position our identities among the stars and suns and moons. Some religions see our identities as inborn manifestations of a unique soul.

But whoever we are, our names are the first signifier of our identity. I was born Elizabeth Claire Baranowski, but right after birth I became "Boo-Boo," a nickname given to me by my dad, who thought I looked like Boo-Boo from the Yogi Bear cartoons. The second oldest of eight children to Ellen and Carl, I was the little sister to Jessica and, sixteen months later, big sister to Zachary. I was the grandchild of Robert and Barbara Boyce, and Theoful and Barabara Baranowski. I was given my mother's initials ECB. Elizabeth, she said, like in the Bible. Claire for her middle name. And our last name, a Polish inheritance from my grandfather Teoful Boleslaw Baranowski. It was a name my grandfather hated, because he thought it was too long and too ethnic. So my grandfather refused to give my father a middle name. "Baranowski" was already too much of a burden. These were the relationships that were bequeathed to me at birth. The tangle of my identity.

We cannot choose who we are born as. And rarely can we choose who raises us and how. But we can change our names. There is no official tally of how many people change their names. Many name changes happen upon divorce or marriage. Some happen because a trans person renames themselves to align better with their gender identity. People who were descended from enslaved persons sometimes change their last names away from the name given to them by the enslavers. But each of these chosen names are manifestations and indicators of our identities. They are not only who we want to be, but who we aspire to be.

Which is why, in eighth grade, I changed my name. Growing up in Texas in the 1990s, there were a lot of Elizabeths, and there still are. The name has been consistently popular for the past one hundred years or more. After all, Elizabeth is in the Bible; there are two British queens with that name. Some Elizabeths are Beths, others Liz, rarer still the Betsy. There is a riddle my grandma Boyce used to recite: "Elizabeth, Elspeth, Betsy and Bess / They all went together to seek a bird's nest. / They found a bird's nest with five eggs in, / They all took one, and left four in." The answer is they were all the same person. Elizabeth is a name that is adaptable. But I wanted to be different than all of them. And so I became "Lyz."

Once, many years later, when I was working as an editor for the AOL relationships website, a commenter noted the spelling of my name. (I also moderated the comments.) "Lyz? What kind of name is that?" they said. "You are just someone who needs to be special." I laughed. The commenter had meant to be mean but was correct. Of course I wanted to be special. We all want to be special. As one of eight children, I longed for my own identity.

In *Anne of Green Gables,* Lucy Maud Montgomery's

character Anne Shirley fastidiously makes people spell her name with an E—a dedication to nomenclature that I found inspiring as a young girl. She was not a plain Ann. She was Anne with an E. An Anne adorned. An Anne crowned with a vowel. A woman with a flourish. This is how I came up with the idea to put a Y in my name. It would be superfluous and indulgent. Once, as Anne contemplates her name, a boring old simple name, she notes, "I read in a book once that a rose by any other name would smell as sweet, but I've never been able to believe it. I don't believe a rose WOULD be as nice if it was called a thistle or a skunk cabbage."

I tried to imagine who I would be if I was named Lavender, Lola, Lilac, Rainbow, or Antoinette. In my journal, I marked the changing of my name from Elizabeth to Lyz as a bold romantic statement of identity. "This is who I am now. A Lyz with a Y is not a usual girl. She is an unusual girl," I wrote in April 1997.

This was the same year I began using my babysitting money to buy clothes from Goodwill. Gone were the long jean skirts of my homeschooled youth. I now wore turtlenecks and boxy sports jackets so I could look like Whitney Houston in *The Preacher's Wife*. Or long lacy knit sweaters with wide necklines that showed my collarbones so I could look like Whitney Houston in *Waiting to Exhale*. If identity is something we are born into, it is also something we create. Identity is a constant negotiation and discovery, something we concoct from the raw material of our lives.

A 1999 Harvard University study looked at how young professionals grew into their roles, and put forth the idea of the provisional self—the created identity a person learns to inhabit in order to find success at a job. Participants tried various ways of inhabiting their provisional selves. One method was simply cosplaying as a different person, the person they wanted to be. Another method involved a mixture of old and new selves. All in all, the study found, "By rehearsing these clumsy, often ineffective, sometimes inauthentic selves, they learned more about the limitations and potential of their repertoires and thus began to make decisions about what elements to keep, refine, reject, or continue to search for." By trying on new names, I was seeking an identity to inhabit, someone who could be the version of myself I most fully wanted to be. But the problem was, I didn't know who that was. All I knew is that I didn't want to be Elizabeth.

This possible self is who we are creating as children when we stare in the mirror and put on our mother's makeup, when we swap clothes with our roommates, when we dye our hair or add piercings to our bodies. And this Lyz was my provisional identity, someone I did not yet know, but was a person I wanted to be. Lyz was unique. I was myself. And yet, as I discovered years later, when I first put my name in a search engine, I wasn't that unique. There were a few other Lyzs.

I didn't want to change my last name when I got married. I was always going to be a Baranowski. Growing up with so many siblings feels like being a finger on a hand. You can wiggle on your own, but you are always part of a greater whole. I told my fiancé as we discussed wedding plans that this was who I was: Lyz Baranowski. It was the name I had my first piece published under, a column for my college paper that had been reprinted in a textbook, which had come with fifty dollars and the thrill of realizing that maybe I could be a writer.

But he pushed back. It was impractical, he told me. We needed to be a family. We'd have kids eventually. Families had one last name. I pointed out his aunt had kept her last name. He rolled his eyes. Yeah, but her kids had their father's last name. It was a pointless feminist gesture, he argued. Plus, this was important to him. Didn't I want to be a family?

And so, like most women who get married to a man, I gave up my name. I made the first of many compromises about who I was and what my identity would be because I was in love, and because he was right—what about our kids? And it was my choice, wasn't it?

When I was young, little girls grew up knowing that one day their last name will be gone—that if they are successful at love, their identity, their whole sense of self, will be erased. At the age of fourteen, I thought Lyz DiCaprio had a lovely ring to it. I didn't know it at the time, but the actor I was in love with has a predilection for dating younger women, and by the time I turned twenty-five, I'd be about his age range. My daughter who is in middle school reports the practice is still alive and well, with her friends writing their names as Mrs. Pedro Pascal in their school binders. If you are lucky enough, we tell little girls, if someone loves you enough, he will take away your identity and give you his.

In America and Britain, most heterosexual married women still take the last names of their husbands. The figures are imprecise because name changes happen for many reasons besides marriage, but most estimates put the number at 80 percent. In a 2020 article for the BBC, Simon Duncan, a professor in family life at the University of Bradford in the United Kingdom, who has been researching the practice, notes, "It is quite surprising . . . [so many women adopt the man's name] since it comes from patriarchal history, from the idea that a woman, on marriage, became one of the man's possessions." Duncan notes that despite the fact that legally a woman does not become a man's property upon their marriage—not anymore at least—women still take part in this practice. Despite women's protestations, the reasons they change their names are still steeped in patriarchy and ideas about what a good family is.

The concept of last names is a relatively recent historical invention; they are not even universally used. For centuries when communities and villages were small and relatively isolated, it was easy enough to distinguish John with the red beard from John the butcher. These identifying monikers could be physical descriptions, occupations, the father's name, the mother's name, or geographical locations. My own maiden name, Baranowski, means son of Baranow, a town in southern Poland. These name designations were numerous and often shifted from one generation to the next. For example, in Spain, sons took the names of their fathers as their last names. For a while, the ancient Romans used a numbering system, but that got confusing. Naming conventions have a long and complex

and specifically regional history. So how did it end up that
Western surnames became a way to swallow up a woman's
identity? Blame it on kings and coverture.

In 1086, William the Conqueror commissioned a survey
of all his lands and a written record of the people in it. The
resulting "Domesday Book" collected all those informal
monikers. For England, and later America, which adopted
English customs, names and property rights were governed
by the feudal law of coverture. Under coverture, no woman
had a legal identity. She first belonged to her father and then
belonged to her husband. In a scholarly article for the journal *Clio*, historians Agnès Fine and Christiane Klapisch-
Zuber write, "The aim of the system was to 'locate the
woman in the family context.' Their names thus identified
women as being positioned between two families, belonging
to one or other depending on the context, the stage of their
life cycle, or the property and legal provisions pertaining to
the document where they are mentioned." In sum, a woman
was defined by her relationships to family.

But not everyone complied. Historian Martha Keil notes
that some family members of successful Jewish business-
women in late medieval Austria took the matronymic. Fine
and Klapisch-Zuber also point out that in the late Middle
Ages, the husbands and children of French noblewomen
took up the mother's coat of arms. The Khasi people of India
are one of the world's last surviving matrilineal societies. But
these are exceptions rather than the rule; in Western society
identity and property come through the father.

In America, it's never been technically against the law

for women to keep their birth names when they got married. But something doesn't have to be against the law in order for women to be punished for doing it. In 1855, when the feminist activist Lucy Stone married Henry Blackwell, she kept her last name. But she was refused the right to vote in an 1879 Massachusetts school board election because she didn't register under her husband's last name. Even in this century, women report difficulty accessing insurance benefits if they don't share a last name with their husband.

The second wave of feminism in the 1960s and '70s worked to undo these norms and assumptions. In 1971, Kathleen Harney, a Milwaukee schoolteacher, married Joseph Kruzel. She continued to use Harney until the school district informed her she had to go by her husband's last name if she wanted to add him to her health insurance. Harney sued to keep her name. She lost. Judge Ralph Podell wrote that he "feels very strongly that family unity also requires that all members thereof bear the same legal name" and "this court feels she should carry her husband's name." It's a sentiment that is still widely held today. Additionally, Podell also noted that married people should have the same last name and if they couldn't agree on one, he added, "it would be better for them, any children they may have, and society in general that they do not enter into the marriage relationship." In a 2021 interview, Harney said that when news of her lawsuit was published in the newspaper her parents stopped speaking to her. But an attorney named Priscilla Ruth MacDougall was also reading the paper and when she saw the news, she contacted Harney and offered to file an appeal pro bono. Harney's appellate lawyer Joan Kessler worked with the ACLU's Ruth Bader Ginsburg on her brief. Ginsburg filed an amicus brief on behalf of Harney in which she used a quote from Shakespeare: "He that filches from me my good name / Robs me of that which not enriches him, / And makes me poor indeed."

"Why, as a condition of marriage," Kessler asked in her brief, "should this state compel one party to the marriage to exact from the other party so dear a price as one's own name? No rational answer suggests itself."

In Podell's defense, his lawyer argued that Harney had been planning on hyphenating her children's names. What was next? Multi-hyphenate grandchildren and so on? The Wisconsin Supreme Court reversed the decision, noting that the law did not require that a woman take her husband's last name. The case reveals the way that judges see themselves as not just upholding the law but enforcing societal norms, even when those norms violate a woman's personhood.

Changing your name is an additional labor that falls squarely on the shoulders of women. Changing my name when I got married required going to the Social Security office and sitting for several hours before presenting my birth and marriage certificates. Then I had to go to the bank with my documents and change my driver's license and passport. I got a new email address and changed my name on all my online accounts. PayPal proved to be difficult to change. I had to fax my birth certificate and make a phone call, and I remember being asked to mail in a notarized document, so I just gave up. Nearly twenty years later, PayPal and eBay are the two places where my birth name remains intact. Then there are the hidden labors of the change—getting new checks, spending hours on hold with credit card companies who seem confused by the changes, as if people weren't marrying every day, and learning a new signature. Mine changed from neat and loopy to a lazy scrawl that seems to have only an L, a squiggly line, an E, another line, then a Z. Everything blending and blurring together. As a journalist I often try to track down sources and internally curse when I have to find a woman knowing only their maiden name. Marriage is how women are disappeared, not just from our online searches but throughout history.

In a study on name changing for the journal *Gender and Society*, sociologists Laura Hamilton, Claudia Geist, and Brian Powell asked survey respondents to talk about why they believed women should take their husband's last names. While respondents gave varying answers, the study's authors note that all the answers relied on looking to outside sources, such as tradition or the Bible, as a guide. And while more liberal respondents focused on choice as an aspect of the decision, the majority of respondents, despite their backgrounds, came to the same place—a wife should take her husband's name.

Sure, a woman may not "have" to change her name, but she wants to for the family, for her husband who she loves so much. And why not just give herself away piece by piece? Never asking why her husband is never asked to make similar sacrifices.

Whenever I talk about taking a husband's last name with other women, the mood can easily get defensive. They did it because they wanted to, and how dare you call them anti-feminist or look at their reasoning. It was a personal decision.

An essay I published in 2021 called out the hypocrisy of "choice feminism" using last names as an example and caused an uproar in the comments section, where women who had changed their names vehemently defended their choice to take their husband's name, not just as an act of love, but as an act of liberation. One woman told me that her family had been abusive, and she wanted to shed herself of that past. Marriage provided the perfect opportunity. I was surprised by the tone of the conversation. My readers are, mostly, sensitive to feminist issues. And there is, of course, no purity test being applied. You cannot be a perfect feminist in a patriarchal world that damns you for one choice and condemns you for another. But the way that last names are still a powerful and personal grip of patriarchy and that we refuse to let go of it is so revealing of how deeply ingrained our own loss of self is.

In these conversations, I asked how hard they'd pushed. Was it really a discussion? Or were they, like me, just wanting to be kind to their partners? Relationships require sacrifice, we tell people, but why, I wanted to know, are women the ones who have to sacrifice their names? Or was it the first in a long line of compromises, ones done in the name of love, that ultimately brought them to a place where they were doing the majority of the housework and childcare, and wondering what the hell had happened to their egalitarian marriage? These are hard questions to ask of ourselves, much less others. Still harder to answer without defensiveness and trying to protect the relationship. I am divorced, I have no relationship to protect, and I can say that I took that last name.

In writing about "choice feminism," author and critic Moira Donegan argues that we like to believe in the idea of a choice, because it allows us to choose subjugation and thus absolve ourselves of the political consequences. It's not anti-feminist to be anti-feminist if a woman so freely chooses. Donegan writes, "In some cases, 'choice' is used to make coercion look like volition. In other cases, 'choice' is used to shield individual women's participation in misogyny from feminist scrutiny. In this way, the weaponization of 'choice' has kept feminists from analyzing women's compromises with patriarchy for what they really are: compromises."

That this relic of patriarchy persists and is reinforced by cultural norms, institutions, and even our legal system shows how deeply we refuse to let go of regressive ideas about gender and its performance.

Names are powerful. Is a person an *immigrant* or are they an *illegal alien*? Is someone *advocating for LGBTQ rights* or are they a *groomer*? Are you a *freedom fighter* or an *insurrectionist*? Do you *fight for justice* or are you just a *woke liberal*? Anne Shirley was right. A rose is not just a rose.

Taking my husband's last name was a powerful symbol, because in his imagination, and in my own, I became something else to him. Something changed. Something his. The process of renaming is a powerful one. It sits at the intersection of gender and race and class and power. When colonial

invaders would conquer a country, they would quickly re-
name the cities, verbally, symbolically, taking control of the
language and the identity. It didn't matter that it was my
choice. I was now a conquered territory.

In her book *All About Love,* bell hooks wrote that true
love cannot be possible under patriarchal systems, because
patriarchy is an imbalance of power. Hooks argues, "Patriarchal masculinity requires of boys and men not only that they
see themselves as more powerful and superior to women but
that they do whatever it takes to maintain their controlling
position." The symbols of patriarchy are still necessary. And
women are told to conform to them, because it's just a name,
silly. It's just a name.

It's also easier to conform than it is to do something different. The author Aubrey Hirsch kept her last name when
she got married and gave her children her last name. She
wrote about it in an essay for *Time* that chronicled the backlash she received on social media for that decision. The essay
generated even more backlash, because, as it turns out, it's
not just a name but the very heart of how we conceptualize
family and male power.

Hirsch wrote:

> Despite the fact that my kids' names have nothing to
> do with them and affect them in no way, dozens of
> people (mostly men) have taken time to share their
> outrage with me, call me names, accuse me of being
> a bad mother or of destroying incentives for men to
> marry, and threaten me for denying a man of his
> birthright to pass on his name. I've seen so many

variations of people asking, "Why would you give the kids your father's last name instead of your husband's?" that, at times, I begun to feel invisible. It's not just my father's name. It's my name. Couldn't they see that erasing a woman's ownership of her own name is a symptom of the same disease I'm trying to remedy?

The backlash Hirsch received reveals that it's not just a name. It's a symbol of power. And when that power is threatened, it lashes out.

The continuation of the human race is predicated on perpetuating patriarchal narratives and false ideas of love that involve a woman giving up her freedom and her name, so she can do unpaid labor for the rest of her life. We have built an entire society with a language of equality but not a practice of it. And any attempt to right that wrong is still met with shock, horror, and outrage.

When I was eighteen, my mother gave me a copy of *Domestic Tranquility*, an anti-feminist manifesto by F. Carolyn Graglia, who argued that the feminist narrative of seeking a career is a failure. Graglia writes that fulfillment in life comes from home and family. Take it from her, she should know. She was a lawyer who quit that life after meeting her husband. And she was happier once she quit. I don't doubt that at all. Capitalism can be just as extractive as marriage. And if you are going to have your labor exploited, it might be easier to do it in a nice home.

But I think the problem is that both narratives are failures. Women dedicating their lives to being cogs in the wheel
of capitalism isn't fulfillment. But neither are home and children. Jobs can be lost. So can homes. Children grow up to
become their own people. And home, children, and marriage,
however much you want them, might not be accessible for
everyone.

In *Inequalities of Love,* Averil Y. Clarke elucidates how
romantic narratives exclude Black women, who are seen
as less desirable as partners by white and Black men. Marriage isn't accessible if men don't want to date you because
you are too Black, too fat, or disabled. It's no accident that
the most prominent spokeswomen for heteronormative, monogamous relationships are white women influencers on Instagram.

I watch these traditional homemakers on social media as
they extol the values of home and being a mama. But in becoming these embodiments of "traditional" womanhood,
these women are actually bucking patriarchal tradition. The
life of social media influencer is a job. It offers validation of
a self-constructed identity outside of marriage and motherhood. It reinforces norms, because it's a lucrative money-
making outlet, but in reinforcing them, bucks them, because
they make money and have identities and success and power.
Even when that power is limited and policed.

"I love just being a mama," writes the influencer formerly
known as Southernish Mama, Brooke Raybould, who has
325,000 Instagram followers and performs motherhood to
her fans. But she's also a business owner. The videos she

makes take time. Promotion takes effort. Her performance of home and family takes an investment. She's not just a "mama"; she's a businesswoman selling you an image, a lifestyle that doesn't exist. She's working at creating the perfect image of the stay-at-home-mama lifestyle, and if she's lucky, and smart, it will be lucrative. I did this myself for a while, writing and taking pictures of my children, writing about parenthood, and making money. The money wasn't that good. Or maybe I wasn't that good at holding together the facade. Making it my job. But it's a little like an ideological pyramid scheme: The hustlers need other women to buy into it, so they can sell them the right strollers, the good kind of diapers, and with it, the perfect performance of marriage and motherhood. It's a kind of grift that will always have a market as long as we need women to give themselves up to romantic partnerships so that they will become the social safety net that our leaders and politicians refuse to create.

But, as women are learning, corporations are not a solution to marriage and gender inequality. Careers can be oppressive, and when combined with the expectation that our jobs be our lives, they can be all-consuming and empty. I began the pandemic encouraging the women in my life not to quit their jobs. "Stay. It's important to work for you and your identity," I'd say.

But as the pandemic dragged on, I was fired from my job—a job that had expected me to take on additional responsibility without any additional compensation, and I had no childcare. I began to shrug my shoulders. "Quit. Whatever." Why should we break ourselves to work within a system not designed for our success? Women are paid less. Mothers are paid even less. The pay gap grows wider for Black mothers, Hispanic mothers, and people who identify as LGBTQ. Women are told to ask for promotions and raises like their male counterparts do, but when they do, they are denied them. Companies that call us family don't compensate men and women equally or offer paid parental leave. And forget about affording childcare. A *Glamour* survey found that one in three women have stayed in an unhappy relationship because they didn't have the money to leave. A culture that underpays women and puts them at a financial disadvantage is a culture that forces women into economic dependence and traps them in unhappy marriages.

What else is possible? What other lives? What other modes of meaning and being? What other ways of living, of being a family, of finding joy are there outside of the binary?

I thought I could do it. I thought I could be myself, independent and whole, and change my name. I thought I could be in an equal partnership and be a mother. I was wrong. Not because I didn't try hard enough, but because the entire system was rigged against me. And I should have recognized that the moment I gave up my name just to make our marriage work.

That's the hardest thing about divorce: It's the most public way of saying you were wrong. And I was wrong. And in his defense, my husband never pretended to be anything other than what he was.

When I divorced, everyone asked me if I would change my name. I thought about it. But I wasn't Lyz Baranowski anymore, even if I wanted to be. I told people that if I were being honest, I'd just change my name to Lyz, simply Lyz. Like Prince or Madonna. A wholly new kind of person. But I keep my married last name. It's part of me now. I am both product of patriarchy and someone who pushes against it. I took his name, and I made it my own.

I need to change the name on my bank account. So, I am ushered into a small office to meet with a banker. On her desk is a small bag filled with rose quartz. Rose quartz, she tells me, is a symbol of love and relationships, and she hands them out to women because she wants them to know they are loved. She's a single mother of five children. She doesn't date anymore. She's trying to go back to school. Ten years ago, her husband just stopped coming home. He told her that he wasn't having fun anymore. She had four kids then, and her oldest was eight. "Imagine it not being fun with four small kids!" she says. "It's, like, *no one* was having fun." She shrugs. It worked out. She was mad for so long. But then she realized she was free. He did her a favor by disappearing. She feels bad for the people who have to co-parent—still managing the volatile feelings of their ex. But this is just life. She tells me every woman she knows is like us. We all have at least one marriage under our belts. It's natural like stone. She laughs and hands me a rose quartz.

5

The Heterosexual Repair Project

One year into our marriage, my husband and I purchased a house. Together, we were quickly checking off the boxes of functional American adulthood. First, we'd gone to college. Then, we'd gotten married. Now it was time for a house.

The house was built in 1925 and had arched doorways with oak crown molding and glowing hardwood floors. The dining room had an original glass chandelier. The kitchen included a cozy built-in nook, and the backyard had a weeping cherry tree that in May looked like a waterfall of pink flowers. The house also had the pervasive smell of must seeping up from the basement. And sure, the bathroom hadn't been updated since 1954, and was there a radon problem? Absolutely. But our realtor told us it would be simple to fix it up. No problem. And we believed her.

I should have known better. I had watched as my parents

struggled to renovate that Victorian in South Dakota, cough-
ing up drywall dust and falling through the floorboards for
years. So it was my fault. I was the one who knew better and
still wanted an old house.

The realtor had tried to show us newer homes in the area
where all the young professionals lived. But I refused to go
see them. If I had to live in Iowa, I wanted to live in the part
of town with the crooked porches, the big trees, and sighing
roofs. I hated the smooth reliability of vinyl siding and the
lifeless beige walls of new construction. Where was the history? Where were the built-ins? Where were the ghosts?

Homeownership has always been a key part of the American
Dream as well as a mechanism by which those in power re-
inforce existing hierarchies and exclude certain people from
prosperity. A woman could not take out a line of credit on her
own until the 1970s. But it wasn't until the 1980s that courts
ruled husbands don't have the right to take out a second
mortgage on their homes without consulting their spouse.
Women have been systemically sidelined from property ownership for centuries, meaning that wealth stays in the hands
of the primary property owners—men. Recent data shows
that homeownership among single women is at 19 percent,
8 points higher than among single men. And while this is
encouraging, studies show that women pay more for those
houses. Experts believe this is because of the gender pay
gap. Women earn less than men, and single women tend to
have fewer assets, and thus have a higher income-to-debt
ratio on average. This ratio is what is used to calculate the

mortgage rate, which means women pay more for mortgages. And this puts women at a structural disadvantage.

For Black families and Black women in particular, the disparity in homeownership is even worse. Historically, Black people have been pushed out of homeownership. In 1933, the new Federal Housing Administration, which was established as a New Deal program to fix the housing crisis, denied mortgages and homes to Black families. It wasn't better after WWII. Black men had a difficult time cashing in on the promise of advancement from the GI bill. In 1947, only two of the more than 3,200 VA-guaranteed home loans in thirteen Mississippi cities went to Black borrowers. Historians Ira Katznelson and Suzanne Mettler write that it wasn't much different elsewhere: "In New York and the northern New Jersey suburbs, fewer than 100 of the 67,000 mortgages insured by the GI bill supported home purchases by non-whites." Today, disparities in home appraisals and bank loans still make homeownership more difficult for Black families.

Homeownership has been one of the primary ways that wealth is accrued in America. Someone who has the down payment can buy a home, and in many places in America, a mortgage can be less than rent. So not only does the homeowner save on monthly bills, but after a few years, the home will usually appreciate in value and the owner can sell it for a profit. Or this was how it was supposed to work until the 2008 recession and the housing crisis turned that logic on its head. Families, mostly lower income, were lured into homeownership with deceptively low interest rates and low monthly payments but were suddenly unable to make their mortgage payments as interest rates rose and home values plummeted.

For my husband and me, our homeownership did not come about through our bootstraps, grit, or determination. It was because my husband's parents gave us the money for the down payment. That was it. We had also moved to Cedar Rapids, Iowa, where houses were relatively affordable, often hundreds of thousands of dollars less than in the Twin Cities.

The house we bought wasn't my first or second choice. Or even my third. I wanted a bungalow, with a sloping floor that my husband insisted was evidence the entire house would collapse in on itself. (The house is still standing.) When we found the one we would eventually buy, I was willing to hold out. I didn't love the musty smell and I wanted built-in bookshelves. But he insisted this was the one. And it was a bargain—an expired listing the realtor had dug up.

The only bathroom with a working shower was in the basement, a cheap plastic one full of mold. Taking a shower in there was like trying to get clean inside a cave. The upstairs bathroom had a shower but no vent, and the tile was cracked and falling off the walls. I wanted to immediately begin remodeling the upstairs bathroom, but my husband insisted we would instead smooth out the dining room walls. The walls were plaster and, like any old house, were a little uneven on the surface. It seemed like a silly project. But what did I know? He was the engineer—a fact he frequently brought up when we had these arguments. He was not a structural engineer or even a civil one. His specialty was electrical engineering. But a common trait of engineers is they feel like they can fix absolutely anything.

Two months into homeownership, my husband was putting drywall joint compound on the cracks in the plaster in the dining room. He'd been at it for days: sanding, then mudding, then sanding again. I'd pointed out that they were superficial cracks. They happened in old homes. We'd just paint. It would be fine. But no, he assured me. I knew nothing.

He didn't tape up plastic over the doorways, so fine white dust filled the house. It was on everything, inside everything. It would settle on our faces as we slept, and I'd wake up feeling grimy. I washed our sheets every two days. Even after I eventually taped up plastic over the doorways, the dust filled in the cracks of our beautiful wood floors. For years, until we redid the floors, I would scrub them on my hands and knees using a toothbrush and a putty knife to try to get the white dust out.

We had a shop vac then—a particularly useful appliance that should be handed out to everyone once they start living on their own. I would support an entire political party that was just about getting shop vacs into the hands of every American over the age of twenty. The shop vac would have been helpful in mitigating this mess. But the shop vac sat unused in the corner of the dining room.

I did not want to clean up. This was his mess after all. I would not do it. But he didn't either. And the dust drifted up against the walls like piles of sand on a beach. My husband began to get nosebleeds from the dust. One night, as he packed up work for the night, I asked him why he didn't clean up.

"There will just be more dust," he said.

"But the dust is everywhere!" I was furious.

I'd been trying to go along. I'd been trying to relax and

not nag. But I was sick of tasting dust in the back of my throat. I was sick of dust covering my clothes, my food. I wanted a bathroom that I could get clean in.

I angrily grabbed the shop vac and turned it on. I didn't know that he had, for some reason, reversed the hose. A huge fog of white powder blew up around me. I slapped the off button. And then I sat down on the floor and cried.

My husband laughed. "It's the fog of war," he said. I laughed, too, because I wanted to be a good sport. I wanted to be the kind of chill wife that just let things go. So I laughed. Years later, that story was one I'd tell at parties. *Look at us, so young and stupid.*

That house was our home, which meant that everything we did with it felt significant: Every tile, every wall, was part of our relationship. And sure, there were problems—the radon, the musty smell, the water pressure—but the bones were good. We just needed to do the work.

Eventually, my husband's attempt to replaster the walls ended and we disagreed on whether the enterprise was a success or if it had been a waste of time. We considered it a draw, and moved onto the upstairs bathroom, which needed new tile and a ceiling vent for the shower. He and I had spent hours on YouTube, going through the steps and researching. We could do it. It would be easy. We just needed to take out the old tile and put in a vent. Easy. But nothing in old homes is ever easy.

Two weeks into the project, the entire bathroom had

been ripped down to the studs, and we were barely speaking to each other.

What happens if you have an old bathroom that people have been using without a proper vent? Mold. There was mold behind all the tiles, mold seeping into the plaster and the lathes. Mold everywhere. So together we demolished the walls, ripping everything apart. Destruction is the easy part. Taking a crowbar to something someone else has built and ripping it down to its most basic elements involves little more than raw force. Destruction is a delight. Anything can be destroyed. And anyone can do demolition. But repair takes skill. Repair takes time. And repair takes a knowledge of what can be fixed and what should be razed to the ground.

The moment the bathroom was demolished, we disagreed on how to rebuild. I wanted to haul away the old tub, which was nothing special, and remake the bathroom all in gleaming white: subway tiles on the walls and white herringbone on the floor. My husband wanted it done cheap. We went to Home Depot and spent hours arguing over tile. Once, as we talked in sharp hushed voices, a couple in their fifties rounded the corner. "Sorry," I said, addressing them. "Bathroom renovations."

The woman laughed and pointed her thumb at the man with her. "This guy once had our bathroom out of commission for three whole years."

I gasped. My husband laughed. "See, it could be worse." I had to give him that: Other men were probably much, much worse.

We settled on a brown stone tile and purchased drywall.

I had wanted to hire someone to hang it. My husband said no, he'd do this. And I'd help. But as we hung the drywall, I noticed the boards were not lining up. The wall studs were warped. I pointed this out and he told me it was my fault, I was too weak, I couldn't press the board close enough to the wall. I insisted the studs were warped; it was an old house. The fight escalated until he asked me, what did I know about fixing a home? I told him I knew just as much as he did.

It's hard to tell the truth about a marriage. We are, most of us, loyal to our loves. Revealing all the hundreds of tiny horrors, the everyday indignities, feels disloyal. I had a friend who was a pastor's wife who would stop any conversation that devolved into frustrations about husbands by raising her hand for silence and say, "Are you tearing him down or are you building him up?" As if speaking the truth about him refusing to wash the bathtub was worse somehow than him actually refusing to wash the bathtub. Speaking those small betrayals makes them real, makes them problems you have to deal with. Even now, I remember the tiny things I hid with little excuses or jokes. But now I want to tell as much of the truth as I can. I want to be completely honest in a way I could not be if I had stayed. Telling the truth is often a demolition project.

A woman who runs a Facebook group for single divorced mothers told me in an interview, "Don't write about divorce; no one wants to hear a negative woman." After my divorce was public, a woman in the town where I live, a former neighbor, herself divorced, emailed me about how to behave post-divorce, instructions that included never talking about my ex at all. An art professor in the nearby town of Mount Vernon served me wine and hummus and told me about her art installation that was about her divorce from another art professor and how he sent a cease-and-desist letter. How her friends urged her to just be quiet about it all. And "it all" in this situation was the multi-year affair he had while she raised their daughters. Let the past be the past, people told me. Don't look in the rearview mirror. Keep going forward. I've always hated that metaphor. Because looking behind you is an essential part of driving. If a car you are driving hits something, you look in the rearview to see what it was. You pause. You assess. You pull over to take care of the damage. That's what no one wants to do. We are a nation of hit-and-runners. We don't want to deal with the consequences.

So many marriages are built on intentional ignorance—the things we refuse to acknowledge. The rot we tile over, letting it hide in the walls until it takes over. I once read about a home that a couple inherited from the wife's family. When they went to renovate the kitchen, they discovered the floor was covering a three-hundred-year-old well. They needed to do thousands of dollars of extra work. One of their ancestors had just put cheap floorboard over that well, leaving the problem for someone else. Letting the damp accumulate until it almost destroyed the home.

When we'd been married for seven years, I organized a Mother's Day fundraiser for a local nonprofit and invited writers and activists to perform monologues on motherhood.

One performer, who would later become a local politician, spoke about being raised by two mothers.

I was pregnant and had one child at the time and very little childcare, and I was struggling to organize the fundraiser. My husband refused to help. He was silent and recalcitrant about the whole ordeal until, one night, we had a fight about it. He didn't approve of what I was doing; he didn't want me promoting gay marriage. His words felt like a slap.

I was stunned and embarrassed. I was married to someone who hated gay marriage? Did he hate my friends? The people I loved? How had I gotten here? How had I failed to see the truth? I organized the fundraiser anyway, bringing my toddler along to rehearsals. We raised $5,000, and it was a huge success. He never came to the show and when people asked why, I told them he was sick. I never told anyone what he believed until my marriage was long over. Then, I told one dear friend, one who had been to our wedding. "Oh, honey, he actually believes that?" she said. "You can't sustain a relationship with someone like that."

I had known she'd say that, which is why I never said anything when we were married. I had covered up the dark well with cheap floorboard. Fixed. Repaired and painted over the rotting walls. This house would be a good home, I believed. This house would be a beautiful home. But honesty can wreck more lives than a crowbar.

Repairing an old house is a lesson in all the things the previous owners hid. Moving a dishwasher reveals that someone tiled over laminate flooring and laminated over beautiful hardwood. Moving a shelf reveals layers of paint, pastels and orange to gray. Taking down a drop ceiling reveals rotting joists. Taking out a toilet reveals years of water damage. The dramatic tension of HGTV repair shows is based on the surprises that contractors find. The sewage buildup. The raccoons' nest. Those hidden damages. A home cannot be fully repaired until you take out all that is rotting. You have to find all that is broken structurally and put in something newer, something better. You have to decide what repairs are essential and what can wait. You have to ask yourself every day: What are we tearing down and what are we building up?

In her book *Repair,* Elizabeth Spelman wrote that the home is a multipurpose repair shop. It is both a literal place that needs repair, and the place where we retreat to heal and hide our wounded hearts and sometimes wounded bodies. It's where small children return for a Band-Aid for a scraped knee. It's where older children retreat to find safety. And in cases of violence, the home is the silent witness to our breaking. Keeping the secrets we hold. She wrote, "To the extent to which women become the repairers of choice in the household—including being healers of rifts, menders of hearts—there are dangers both for them and for the other members of it. It is a crucial part of a relationship for those in it to be able to tend to its cracks and fissures themselves, to not turn automatically to a third party for a rescue operation."

Homes are repair shops. They are the places where we are fighting entropy. Yet, some repairs are beyond our control.

And so there we were. It was nine P.M., and my husband and I were standing in a ripped-up bathroom, floorboards exposed, drywall leaning against the wall outside the door. I come from a family of fighters. Of shouters and yellers. He comes from a family of silences. Of coughs and side glances. And I was telling him this wasn't working. The bathroom repair isn't working. I was telling him we are going to have to do it all over again.

He was red-faced. His voice was soft but furious. He didn't trust me to measure. I'm imprecise. I didn't take advanced calculus like he did. I'm incapable of knowing what he knows.

"Stop treating me like an idiot. I'm your partner here. We are doing this together."

"I don't want your help," he said.

I walked out of the bathroom. And then out of the house. I got into the car and I started driving. I would go somewhere. Anywhere. I wouldn't come back. I drove to Barnes & Noble and sat drinking coffee until they closed. Then, I sat in the parking lot crying.

Why didn't I go to a bar and have a drink? Why didn't I drive to Minneapolis and stay with my friends? I think about this now. I wonder if there is a different version of myself, one who walked out that night, one who understood this couldn't be fixed. One who got free. But that version of me did not exist back then. My parents had taught me marriage was hard. You had to work at it. You just had to keep trying to fix it.

I will hear this advice over and over again. Repeated ad nauseam from the pulpit and prestige publications, like *The Atlantic,* where Arthur Brooks chides couples to see marriage not as a "me" but a "we" and not to get all caught up on who is doing more of the work, because sometimes marriage is like that. You just have to work. But whose work? Who is responsible for the repair and maintenance of a marriage? Who buys the self-help books? Who goes to the conferences and pushes their partner into therapy? In a 2019 study, sociologist Allison Daminger found that women carry the majority of the cognitive load in their relationships. Meaning women are the ones noticing, analyzing, and monitoring the issues in a marriage. Daminger broke down the concept of mental load into four parts: anticipating, identifying, deciding, and monitoring. The aspects of cognitive load where Daminger noticed that women do most of the work was in anticipation and monitoring. Women are thinking of the problems, working to solve them, and monitoring them for success.

This is the unspoken reality of fixing a home or fixing a relationship. Yes, it is hard work. But the labor mostly falls on women. It's women buying the self-help books and making the couple's therapy appointments. It's women making the date nights and hiring the sitters and making the dinner reservations. It's women doing the repairs.

When I drove home that night and walked in the door, I knew what our roles were supposed to be. He would repair the walls. And I would repair our relationship. I arrived at the house just after midnight and crawled into bed. We never spoke of the fight again. Once the drywall was up, I used a faux stucco paint to cover up the lumpy, uneven wall. I hate fake stucco but it was the only thing that covered the imperfections. But eventually, water stains leaked through the drywall. I will never know what they were. When I pointed them out to my husband, he told me they were nothing and to just put more paint over them. But no matter how much paint I used, large discolorations bloomed on our new walls.

Five years into our relationship, my husband and I began watching the show *Fixer Upper,* hosted by the American sweethearts of the HGTV industry, Chip and Joanna Gaines. The premise of the show is that the Gaines assist another couple in buying and renovating a home in Waco, Texas. *Fixer Upper* has been a huge success, and the Gaineses have created a home repair empire. Joanna's spin-off rustic chic home design company Magnolia is now sold in Target. Home prices in Waco have increased nearly 10 percent each year from 2017 to 2021—an effect that local realtors attribute to the Gaineses.

We watched the show as we renovated our own home. The Gaineses' relationship is the perfect model of the American ideal of marriage. They work together as business and romantic partners. Chip is a gruff, handsome, goofy handyman, who does the dirty work. Joanna is pretty and polished and responsible for making the homes beautiful. Chip is silly. Joanna is responsible. The couple has a brood of charming well-dressed children. The show works because the Gaines ethos of renovation is not a complete revamp, or an unrecognizable transformation. You won't find modernist design or modular furniture. It's budget friendly, family friendly, and homey. And each home they renovate is older. They are repairing the past.

The couple uses a lot of shiplap—a wooden board common on barns and sheds and outbuildings—and reconstructed barn-type doors inside of the homes. Their aesthetic fe-tishizes the farmhouse of the past; it's an American tradition-alist ideal. So, too, does the relationship they model. Joanna is strong, physically and emotionally, but still accommodat-ing to her husband. She rarely challenges him, and when she does, it's gently deferential. Chip is the heavy laborer, mas-culine in everything he does. Like their designs, the couple's relationship does not challenge traditional gender roles; it only polishes them up, renovates them, and makes them pal-atable for a whole new generation.

I hated the show. I dubbed it "Hobby Lobby chic." It was manufactured authenticity. New floorboards distressed to look old. White-toothed, heavily edited, relational happiness performed on-screen.

Once, when irritated with my running commentary, my husband told me I was jealous. And he wasn't wrong. I was envious of how well the Gaineses' relationship seemed to work. How beautiful the homes they created were. Our home smelled. Its damp, musty scent burrowed into our hair and clothing. I would spray down the basement walls with bleach every week and open the windows trying to cut down on the smell, but it permeated our clothes. I never got used to it. It was especially bad after a weekend away, when I'd walk into the house and the smell would hit me like a wall. My stomach would curl up in nausea. My husband claimed it wasn't that bad. He told me I smelled fictional smells. Years later, after I moved out, after a couple of drinks, two dear friends would sheepishly confess how much they hated the smell of that house.

Compared to the Gaineses, our renovations were sloppy

and haphazard. The tile in the bathroom hadn't been sealed properly, and I spent my Saturday mornings scrubbing the floor with a variety of different cleansers and DIY solutions that promised to clean my grout. They never worked. The bits of dirt always remained. Mold soon bloomed on the newly finished bathroom walls, and I dutifully scrubbed them twice a week. But the mold always came back. I used a putty knife to dig the plaster dust out from between the floorboards, but it never looked clean enough. I'd go to garage and estate sales to buy furniture and home décor, cleaning everything, spray-painting it to find new life. But it never seemed to fit.

And hadn't I—an educated woman, one who'd rejected the conservative model of her upbringing, one who'd marched in "Take Back the Night" rallies and written about sexual assault in the college newspaper, and been Phi Beta Kappa—well, hadn't I chosen this life?

While I was watching *Fixer Upper,* all my friends were watching *Girls,* the critically acclaimed show written by and starring Lena Dunham, which follows an aspiring writer and her friends in their exploits around New York City. The show is good, but when I tried to watch it, I felt it was set on another planet. Here I was in my twenties, buying throw pillows from flea markets and pricing out granite countertops, while those girls were talking about dating and sex and designer shoes and other things that had no relevance to my life. But here was this couple on HGTV performing a version of my life—a couple renovating a home on a budget. Chip and Joanna were supposed to be the perfect model of building a home and a life together, metaphorically and physically. And I hated it.

HGTV shows, YouTube videos, blogs, and Instagram influencers are filled with couples who with power tools and a little bit of paint renovate and rebuild the physical embodiment of the American family: the home. Sometimes they fight. The "oh, we disagree" joking posts happen. But never the screams. The slamming doors. The bathtub in the basement for three years. Or the toes broken on power tools left on the floor in the middle of the night. On HGTV, the fights, just like the homes, are always fixable. And watching them I always wondered what would happen two or three years later. Was the grout done sloppily and would mold grow behind the tile? Were the bookshelves installed improperly and would they fall off the wall? Was the wiring bad? Which rooms did we not see? And which couple would see their home redone only to have their marriage fall apart?

When I was pregnant with our first child, my husband decided to strip down all the wood trim on the second floor. The thinking was that the wood on the first floor was lovely, so perhaps he could restore the painted trim on the second floor. I objected to the project, because I could think of ten other projects that had to get done first. The dank-smelling basement perhaps? Plus, I was pregnant and I was worried about the chemical fumes from wood stripper and paint. But the project went ahead. After our bathroom fight, I had come home and ceded the world of power tools to him. That was how we were going to get through this: if I stayed in the lane he designated for me, and he stayed in the one he paved for himself.

So he began sanding and grinding. And one night, as I walked to the bathroom to pee, I tripped over a power tool left on the floor and broke my toe. In the morning, my foot bruised and throbbing, I told him, "You did this!"

"Turn on the lights next time," he said. In the end, the entire project was canceled because he discovered the wood underneath was cheap old trim. Exactly the kind you cover up with paint. I was in charge of repainting.

Did I ask for that job? Or did I just take it on? No one, of course, demanded that I do it, not in so many words. I could have chosen not to live in a home that smelled, had walls that were crooked, left the trim with its mottled streaks of half-stripped wood. I could have chosen not to buy the throw pillows and scrub the dust out of the floors. No one told me to spend hours and hours in Home Depot and then Target, buying decorations and cleaning supplies. No one told me to Google "how to clean grout" or "how to get rid of musty basement smells" at two A.M. I simply did it. I did it so my home would be nice. So that my house would be good. So that my life would be happy. But one of the most important parts of a repair job is recognizing when something is irreparable.

I was married to an engineer, a man who believed that he had the ability to fix anything. Whose confidence in that fact permeated every aspect of our home. There was nothing he would call in an expert on. If there was a problem, there was a technical fix for it that he himself knew. But fixing something restores what is old. It's a conservative effort. It is an act of holding together the past. But if all that is holding a home together is the labor of one person, that house cannot stand.

———————

I'm in a bar in St. Paul, Minnesota, grabbing dinner after a day of following a politician around for a story. A woman sits next to me and asks me about my work. I tell her I am writing a book about divorce, about how America uses marriage as the social safety net. How marriage is a partnership based in inequality. I normally don't say all of that. Normally, I just say the book I'm working on is about marriage, and leave it at that. But I'm tired and my ex has sent me an email lecturing me because I told our daughter she could quit dance. He doesn't think anyone should quit anything, apparently. And I'm tired and irritated. So I tell this woman the truth.

She is divorced and tells me about it. How it was relatively easy. They'd been married for five years and she woke up and realized she didn't have a life that she wanted to live in. They had no children and it was amicable. Their divorce, as she described it, sounded just like a leaf falling from a tree. A natural departure. She wonders sometimes if maybe he was in love with someone else. But she doesn't care. "Leaving," she tells me, "it's the best part of living."

———————

6

The Easy Way Out

I n 2017, my friend Matthew moved to town with his kids for a job teaching writing at a local college. His wife was in Korea where she was receiving experimental cancer treatments that he hoped would save her life. We knew she was dying, but we still spoke with hope. I'd never met her, but she hovered like a spirit as I helped Matthew move in and unpack. As our children played together, he and I drank wine on his deck.

My marriage was dying, too. I was clinging to hope. But I was exhausted. I was trying to write my first book. And each time I planned a research trip I'd have to make meals in advance, plan childcare, organize the schedule. It was so much work.

One early summer day, we sat on the deck, fingers greasy from Popeyes, watching our older girls chase our little boys. My husband was working late, and I didn't tell him we wouldn't be there when he got home. I told Matthew about my misery and how I wished there was another woman. Something I could point to, some event I could hold on to and say, "This! This! Is why I am allowed to go." Something that would justify my act of selfishness.

Instead, I was just unhappy. I was so unhappy. I had dreams I was drowning, pulled under a green murky water by his hands.

"Is it enough to break my life apart just to be happy?"

"Yes." Matthew said this so simply. So clearly. As if it shouldn't even be a question.

We make women feel brave for sticking it out. For keeping private all the screaming fights, the late nights, the broken cups on the floor, swept up in the morning. We make women feel like they are doing something right for persisting in the lonely drudgery of the American marriage, when the aftermath of the happily-ever-after of the heterosexual marriage is simply negotiating a relationship that is inherently unequal. A relationship made unequal not by accident, but as a function of a society that relies on that inequality to fill in the gaps that it refuses to fund—childcare, eldercare. We do not make women feel brave for making the opposite choice, for walking away from unhappiness.

The spring before I got married, my father-in-law paid for my fiancé and me to go to a marriage conference. He paid for two separate hotel rooms and a night out for a date. The conference was held in downtown Minneapolis, over our college spring break. It was cold. And I forgot to bring my makeup.

In the churn of women and men in the conference center, I felt exposed and ugly.

We sat through lectures by pastors and their wives who told us marriage is hard. So hard. But the key is not to give up. God blesses persistence. God does not care about your happiness. God cares about your holiness. Marriage is not there to make us happy, it's to make us holy. I sat doodling in my workbook until my fiancé kicked me to pay attention. This was about our future.

The speakers divided us. Women in one room. Men in another. In the first of these sessions, a beautiful woman with a hairstyle made possible only by backcombing and Aqua Net told us the story of her marriage. They married just out of college. Her husband was in seminary and she was working as a nurse. I can still hear her voice, so bright and tight, like it was going to shatter. *I would come home and his clothes would be all over the floor and he'd be saying, "Babe, what's for dinner?" It was just that I'd been raised by parents who cared for me, and now, suddenly, I had to be this man's chef, his laundry service, and be grateful when he said thank you. I got so mad. One day, I didn't come home, I just drove to my parents' house and sobbed. Sobbed. My dad drove me back to our home. He told me the secret to a good marriage is simply not getting divorced.*

The women around me laughed.

The moral of the story: You stick with it. No matter what.

A friend told me her parents stayed together while her father was an alcoholic, and he got sober after twenty years and her mom was happy. She got angry when I asked, "Couldn't she have been happier sooner?"

x x x

Three years into our marriage, in 2008, I started working for a love-and-sex magazine. I edited marriage experts who reiterated the same line: Marriage and relationships are treated cheaply. Hookup culture has ruined us. Marriage is commitment. You don't quit. And especially not because you've fallen out of love. Love is a feeling, but marriage is a commitment.

In 2013, *The New York Times* printed a debate between two opinion writers about whether to end no-fault divorce. One of the writers, Beverly Willitt, taking the anti-divorce side, argued that divorcing couples should be required to attend mandatory counseling sessions on the harm of divorce. She argued that the divorce rate was high because of self-centered American culture. But it is still harder to get divorced in America than to get married. Most states have waiting periods for divorces with anywhere between 20 and 180 days before a couple can finalize a divorce. Most states don't have a waiting period for a marriage license, and if they do, it's not longer than three days, except Wisconsin, where it's five days. Also, most marriage licenses don't cost more than a hundred dollars, while divorces can cost far more.

Mississippi is one of two states without a true "no-fault" divorce option. "Irreconcilable differences" is one of twelve legally allowable reasons for a couple to divorce in the state, but it requires that the other partner agree. In a 2017 article about the fight to reform Mississippi's divorce laws, one lawmaker noted that marriage should be difficult to end because it's a "biblical commandment." There are no such barriers to marriage. In fact, even though some states have laws barring marriage for people under the age of eighteen, most of those laws allow exceptions including parental or judicial consent. Only seven states have a minimum age of eighteen with no exceptions. And in the United States, while child marriage is rare, the Pew Research Center estimates that five out of every one thousand individuals ages fifteen to seventeen is married. Entering into a marriage is easy. It's divorce that is hard.

In 2017, I'd been married twelve years, and I was working. I scheduled the therapy appointments. I scheduled the date nights. I hired the babysitters. I sat and watched *Star Trek* and tried to engage in conversation about the complicated culture of Klingons, the only characters that interested me. I learned the names of players on the Minnesota Vikings and all about all those times they barely missed making it to the Super Bowl. I memorized Kirby Puckett's number and I'd watched the entire 1991 World Series highlight reel multiple times. Before he died, my father-in-law loved to greet me at the door of his home with a baseball trivia question. As a way, he'd say laughing, to make sure I belonged in the family.

I'd been working on trying to make my marriage work for so long, I knew how to make his family a pie that they'd all love. I knew the family recipe for chocolate chip cookies by heart. I'd learn how to make lefse, his grandmother's tissue paper hands guiding me as I rolled out the thin dough.

For years, I packed his lunch. Exactly how he liked it. Two slices of wheat bread, the Brownberry brand. Meat and a slice of cheese and honey mustard. He liked the Hy-Vee brand of honey mustard. Carrots. Chips. Sun Chips were the best. And a Dr Pepper. In our first years of marriage, I'd put little notes in there. I'd tell him things I liked about him. I'd write flirty little messages, sometimes scandalous. I'd think, I'd hope, that he would reply. I thought and hoped he'd call me in the middle of the day to say how happy it made him. How much he loved me. He didn't.

When our second child was born, I was too exhausted to keep making the sandwiches, and he told me he thought I didn't love him anymore. No, no, no, I am just so tired, I tried explaining. And I was. I was so tired. I had a toddler. I had a baby boy who did not sleep and wanted only me to hold him. Who screamed when he wasn't near me. Who refused a bottle. Sometimes I'd escape to grocery shop, and my husband would call me with the baby screaming in the background to ask, "When are you coming home?"

Please, I'd beg. Just bring food home one day. Just please. I need help.

"But what if you are already cooking?" he said.

I didn't even know how to reply. His words were so devoid of the experience of my life. Already cooking? As if I was actually doing something more besides putting chicken nuggets into the oven and opening a bag of salad.

Once, when my son was just four months old, I put him down for a nap. Then got my toddler daughter in her room for her rest time. She refused to nap. But I tried to get her settled in her room, so I could have just a few moments with no one touching me, no one needing me.

She was defiant and pooped in her underwear and began screaming. I came upstairs to find poop smeared on the carpet and the baby screaming, too. I started screaming. I screamed so loud, my daughter was scared. And I was scared. And we were all scared of one another. I was terrified of the well of exhaustion and rage inside me. I was scared of how much I wanted to run away. I shut myself in the bedroom and called my husband. "Come home," I sobbed. "Come home."

He did. He got the kids, and I refused to come out of the room until it was the baby's bedtime. I was exhausted, and I simply could not face them. When I eventually came out of the room, he'd fed the children. And there was Chinese takeout waiting for me. I thought *This is good*. I thought *Maybe he sees*. That night, after I put the baby to bed, I scrubbed my daughter's shit off the carpet. And my husband told me I needed to get it together. Maybe, he suggested, I should sleep more. And I realized he didn't see me at all. He'd stepped in at that moment, but the message felt clear: Get yourself together. And get back to work.

He would help. But it wouldn't be a regular thing. *Help* is such a misleading verb. We emphasize the person aiding. *The help. The helpers.* People are thanked for their help. But the verb implies a request, a cry, an appeal for aid. Aid was given, yes, but I didn't want to have to cry out in order to be helped. Help, it seemed, only came when things were dire. When I had reached an emotional limit. When the trash was overflowing and when the carpet was littered with toys and there was toddler shit on the floor and I was sobbing. I wanted to be seen. I wanted my emotional fragility to be seen as much as I wanted the sticky countertops to be seen. And I didn't want to have to break down in order for that to happen. I didn't need help; I needed to not carry it all.

✗ ✗ ✗

In 2022, *New York Times* columnist Tish Harrison Warren decried a culture of divorcing for unhappiness, writing, "I want to normalize significant periods of confusion, exhaustion, grief and unfulfillment in marriage. There's an older couple I know who are in their fifth decade of marriage. They are funny and kind and, by almost any standard, the picture of #relationshipgoals. Early on in our marriage they told us, 'There are times in marriage when the Bible's call to love your enemies and the call to love your spouse are the same call.'"

Life is, of course, not easy, and no one is going to like their partner every day. But Warren's column makes misery in marriage sound like a necessary evil of being partnered with a man. It's not. I refuse to believe that it has to be that way. I have two dear friends who I have known for over twenty years; we fight sometimes and disagree. Between us we've had three divorces and four marriages and three children. Never once have they felt like the enemy to me. And if it is that way, if the experience of being with a man means I hate him for at least a third of our marriage and he hates me, too, I'd rather not have it. No, thank you. There is no benefit to that martyrdom. To me, columns like Warren's sound like the mentality that enables hazing rituals and cults where they sacrifice one of their own every fortnight. I was miserable, so you should be, too. I do not want that curse. I want happiness.

Women love to tell me how they stayed married. Oh, it wasn't easy. It never is. Marriage, after all, takes work. But they stayed. They knuckled down. They did the work. Sure, he didn't help with the kids, but they never expected it. And sure, there were other things, problems, maybe drinking, maybe another woman. But they didn't quit. And now, now forty years later, the kids are gone and they are happy. So happy. Happy if only he'd find something to do now that they were retired and he's just in the house all day. *Ha ha ha.*

They are the mothers of my friends. Neighbors. Acquaintances. They are that chorus of women that exist on the periphery of our lives. Aunts. Cousins. The women who attend your wedding shower. Or baby shower. The friends of your mother. A doctor I met while doing a vaccine trial told me how she never had kids; she was working so much as a doctor. She never wanted them anyway. But marriage, she said, marriage is hard. Being married to a man is not easy. Then, after she drew my blood, she instructed me not to put her in my book. I didn't promise anything.

I wonder, is it really worth it? A 2002 study argued that divorce didn't make unhappily married people happier. Yet, a 2005 study suggests that 74 percent of divorced women report feeling liberated compared to 37 percent of men. Of course, some people regret their divorces. And it's a hard number to measure. People who divorce might regret losing the marriage when they realize they won't find another partner. One study that looked deeply at regrets found education and career were the two biggest regrets people had. The third was romance.

At what point is the misery worth it? And do people just say it was worth it, so we don't have to admit that we wasted our lives?

In 2020, I wrote an essay for *Glamour* about how I had to divorce to find equality. Women filled my DMs to tell me how miserable they are, but then said this is just what marriage is. How they persisted for the children. *For the children.* And, well, because being divorced must be lonely; aren't I lonely? Here is the truth: I have never been lonelier than I was when I was on the inside of a miserable marriage.

Some women tell me how they trained their partners. Sure, they came rough and reluctant, but now they do the dishes without complaining. And they'll cook dinner some nights. See? See. Maybe, they imply, if I had tried harder, worked harder, trained my husband, stayed miserable a little longer, I could have stayed married. As if that was the one thing I wanted to spend my time on—training a grown man like a horse.

In the beginning of 2016, I passed out on the bathroom floor while I was getting ready to take the kids on a playdate with a moms group. The group swapped babysitting, and I used the time to work on my book and freelancing. I woke up feeling exhausted with waves of pain going through my back, which was not that unusual. But then a wave of pain washed through me as I was brushing my hair that was so bad I gripped the sink.

When I woke up, I was on the floor and my small daughter had my face in her hands. "Mommy, are you okay? Why you nappin' on the floor? You need bed, Mommy?"

I smiled at her even though I was sweating. "Oh, sorry, honey. I wanted to lie down. Just a bit." I sat up and texted my husband: *Something is wrong, come home. I'm sick.* He didn't respond. I called. He didn't pick up. I called the neighbor. I told her everything, and she said she'd take the kids while I went to the hospital. In between waves of pain, I walked them three houses down, carrying my small son. "This is the playdate today," I said. And in my voice, I was so happy. After I dropped them off, I fell to my hands and knees and vomited in my neighbor's grass. The grass felt cold on my hands. I stared at each individual blade until I could stand again.

He didn't call me for four hours. Long after I'd gone to the ER and learned I had an advanced kidney infection and large cysts in my uterus that were pressing on my spine. Long after I'd been given antibiotics and pain medication and urged not to go home until someone could drive me.

When he called, I answered, but I said nothing.

"How are you?" he asked.

I knew he was concerned. I still said nothing.

"What happened?"

"Come get me," I said. Then I hung up. He did. He brought me home. I napped on the couch. The next day, he took half a day off work. At noon, he looked at me and asked if I was okay.

I said, "Sure. I don't know."

"Okay." And then he left.

As I recovered, my days were waking up, taking my kids to their four hours of morning day care. Coming home, taking a pain pill, napping. Then I picked them up. No pain pills until my husband came home at night and the kids were in bed.

Even after the cysts broke up and the kidney infection healed, I was so tired. My friends made meals, so my husband didn't have to cook. And while I was grateful, I was also furious. I remembered this story whenever I heard a woman say, "I wish I had a man around the house to help."

I want our culture to stop telling women to work harder. In response to news that women receive fewer raises, advice columns tell women how to ask for more money. When statistics show that women are doing more housework, entire industries are developed to show women how to ask their husbands to do more cooking and cleaning. But asking doesn't help. Women *are* asking. It's just that no one is listening.

During the pandemic, whatever progress gender equality had made in American society collapsed in on itself. It was women, wives and mothers especially, who did the bulk of the household work and homeschooling. It's women, and women of color especially, who were being forced out of their jobs because, as the sociologist Jessica Calarco observed, "Other countries have social safety nets. The U.S. has women."

It's worth pointing out that while studies show that women do more housework than their male partners, this work goes largely unobserved by men, half of whom statistically perceive themselves as doing equal work, while only 3 percent of women agree. Add in the fact that husbands add an additional seven hours of labor to a home—labor done by their wives—and it's a bleak picture of domestic partnership. As I write this, op-eds are desperately begging men to take paid leave and to advocate for universal childcare and reproductive rights. I understand; they are written by women who are married and committed to the model. They remind me of the conversations I had in couples therapy, begging for him to vacuum, begging for him to bring food home, begging for help. You shouldn't have to beg. I don't want to spend my life in pain, begging to be seen.

I am fascinated by this gap in work and perception. The answer, I think, lies in that space between the work husbands do and the work they *think* they do. What noticing is lost here? In her book *The Time Bind,* Arlie Russell Hochschild writes that this work is upkeep, it is labor, and much like the work of home repair, it requires "noticing, acknowledging, and empathizing with the feelings of family members, patching up quarrels, and soothing hurt feelings." In sum, the work of a home, of a life, is paying attention. Knowing that the dishwasher drain needs to be cleaned, that the counter is sticky, that the socks need to be matched: It's the work of noticing that isn't being done. And what is lost when the people who love us do not see our labor? It's our happiness.

"'For I hate divorce,' says the Lord, the God of Israel" (Malachi 2:16). This verse was part of our homeschool lessons taught by my mother. God can forgive any sin, but divorce is what he truly hates.

And at church, a sweaty pastor in shirtsleeves, leaning over the pulpit in a brown, brick church in Texas, decried how fast food and convenience culture made divorce the easy way out. Marriage is God's plan. But rumor had it that the pastor was cheating on his wife with the wife of an elder. And my sister Jessie told me it was true; she babysat for the elder's wife and told me, one night, as we lay in our beds, her on the top bunk, me on the bottom. I didn't ask how she knew.

I was ten years old and our dad was coming home late at night. A child insomniac, I would roam the halls after everyone was asleep, and I would catch him, eating ice cream in the kitchen after midnight. He'd been working late, he'd say. And give me some ice cream if I promised not to tell. Later, I learned that these late nights meant betrayal and my parents would pull apart and then come back together, time after time. I lost count, and when I asked, I was told that number was not my business. And maybe not, but it shaped my life.

And so, a pastor who cheated on his wife preached to congregations of miserably married couples about how things were hard. But God wanted us to stay. And as a child the misery made sense. After all, I hadn't ever seen a happy adult. I wasn't being raised to be happy. I was being raised to be good. Those are lessons that are hard to unlearn.

For a long time, I would tell myself, "You won't find anyone better. He's a good man. You think you'll find someone else? You won't."

Single mothers in books and TV shows are all miserable,

overworked and tired, desperately dating, trying to find another happily ever after. I tell my friend Anna all about Shirley Jackson. "She wrote her best while miserable; maybe that will be me."

"I want you to have a better life than that," Anna told me. "I don't think these lives are aspirational."

I left. I'd spent so much of my life being good and following the rules, and I was miserable. I knew all the rules by heart. I'd spent my life in churches listening to men, who had wives who cooked and cleaned for them, theologically debate my right to happiness. The rules, it seemed, had been designed to keep me miserable, always striving for what I was told could never be attained. When I moved out, the amalgamations of all the pastors I've ever heard preach were melded into one small voice, now lodged in my head, telling me yes, this was spirituality. We were always striving, always failing to attain perfection. Life wasn't about our happiness. But why not? Why couldn't I be happy? I wasn't going to play by those rules anymore. I wasn't going to twist and turn my body and my needs so that I could meet that ever-shifting standard of saintliness. I was done. "Praise the Lord and pass the ammunition," sing the Chicks. "I'm arrivin' on a sin wagon."

But this was how I was raised. Believing that marriages don't end. I watched as my parents fought—separating and reuniting. I am old enough now to know that I cannot judge anyone else's choices. When my mother visited me in my new home, I was afraid of her judgment; I was afraid of what she would say. But instead, she turned to me after the children were in bed and said, "I wonder if I had done something different, I wonder, if I had left . . ." And I had to stop her. I could not finish that conversation with her. Because I made my choice. And I am determined to be happy. And isn't that what we're all trying to do?

Talking to my friend Matthew that day, I realized that I had put my happiness in the hands of another person. I'd been waiting for so long for him to see me, to try to make me happy. But no one would ever fight for my happiness or my freedom; that was a battle for me.

In a 1993 interview with *The Paris Review,* Toni Morrison noted of her own ex-husband: "I only know that I will never again trust my life, my future, to the whims of men, in companies or out. Never again will their judgment have anything to do with what I think I can do. That was the wonderful liberation of being divorced and having children."

In *All of This,* Rebecca Woolf writes of her own marriage, which ended when her husband died of cancer, "At the time, I thought I was being brave by sticking it out. By staying together for the kids. But it isn't brave to sit passively in your misery. . . . The bravest women I know are not widows. They are divorced." I'd spent over twelve years asking for someone to give me my happiness. Finally, I stopped asking. I just took it.

This is what people call being selfish. After all, I am a mother, I was a wife. It is my duty to think of others over myself. But what Matthew's simple answer gave me permission to do was to think about myself. And think how, perhaps, if I was happy, if I did every desperate thing I could to grasp for it, maybe I would show my children that life is not misery, and their happiness belongs to them. That their freedom is worth fighting for.

In *The New York Times*, Thessaly La Force wrote a long piece examining the marriages of artists. She writes, "Marriage was, and still is, a conventional route that calcified a certain hierarchy: Wives worked as scheduler and secretary, cook and cleaning lady, even if they had their own books to write, their own sculptures to create or their own paintings to paint."

Imagine, she asks, what would have happened if Susan Sontag had not left Philip Rieff? What if Simone de Beauvoir had married Jean-Paul Sartre? But, she concludes, "Those stories are less fun to tell, they reveal acts of selfishness and cruelty that, though cultivated and rewarded by the idea of male genius, are rarely granted to his counterpart."

My story is one such story of selfishness and cruelty, and it is enormously fun to tell. It's fun, because I know what happens in the end. I know what is on the other side of the breaking, on the other side of screaming because you are so lonely in a rented home that floods every time it rains, on the other side of sobbing on the floor of a basement learning to fix your own washing machine, on the other side of long walks alone in the snow listening to Taylor Swift and wondering what you are doing with this world that you don't know how to behave in, because you are so free, so unencumbered, but also so, so scared.

What happens on the other side is a beautiful house with two dogs and cats and my kids and a porch where I drink coffee, and happiness.

Life, my wise friend Anna told me, is not a game of chicken. You don't have to wait for pain, for misery, for the other person to cheat, to blink first, before you can veer to the side and say, no, I will not play this, whatever silly game this is. Because it's not designed for me to win.

The marriage conference I attended in 2005 happens every year. It's the FamilyLife Weekend to Remember Conference, and their website boasts that couples walk in thinking they will divorce and walk out with a renewed sense of purpose. When I attended with my then fiancé, the pastor giving the keynote address told us that our culture treats marriage as disposable. It's cheap. But marriage shouldn't be something you try on and return to the store, he says.

At the time, I took what he said at face value. Because of course I believed in love. Of course I believed in relationships. I knew that life was hard. I knew it so well, I could not think of a time when life has ever been easy. I was so used to crying about men, working for men, being good for men, that what's another? This was the way of things wasn't it? Wasn't it?

In 1993, *Time* magazine published an article arguing for something called "super vows." Something more ironclad than a normal marriage vow. Something that will keep couples locked into holy matrimony for longer. The author's disdain for what seems like the easy-in, easy-out of marriage "these days" drips from the page.

Twelve years later, in marriage therapy, I thought, who does telling couples that divorce is the easy way out benefit? It benefits the people who don't do the work of making ther-

apy appointments or calling the sitter for date night. That's
who.

There is nothing easy about divorce. Not legally, not emotionally. Because what it requires is burning everything down
to the ground and rebuilding with completely different ma-
terials. It requires sobbing on the floor at two A.M. while your
kids are at their dad's and being so lonely your bones ache. It
requires admitting you were wrong. It requires looking at
your wedding photo and thinking long and hard about what
you thought was the happiest day of your life. It might mean
never seeing your favorite sister-in-law ever again or not
being invited to your nephew's parties. It requires calling a
friend on a Friday and telling her you are lonely and you need
her to get a hamburger with you immediately. It means crying in the Target checkout aisle when a neighbor sees you
buying spatulas and asks you why you are moving. And you
telling her your life is falling apart and her saying, "I've been
there, too." It requires letting go of a dream you once had
about life and love. It means putting yourself first when
everyone tells you that you should be last. It requires learning to reimagine happiness beyond what everyone told you it
should look like.

My divorce journey made me so poor I couldn't go to the
dentist for three years and it ruined my teeth. My parents
gave me money. A friend gave me money. I will never, not
ever, be able to pay them back. People pity single mothers.
"How can you do it?" they asked me. "It must be so hard."
And in the pandemic they asked me this more and more as I

tried to juggle work and homeschool, and I said, actually, it's easier for me because divorce means he has to take the kids at least some of the time. If we were married, it would all be me. I told them husbands add to the housework. I had less of it now. And, more important, I was happy not to be locked inside a home with someone I was at war with.

The secret is that being a single mother is easier because I am not tiptoeing around the demands of a man. Because even though I have children, I have time to breathe, I have time to fuck up. I have time to do stand-up comedy and make mistakes. I have time to cry in my bed. I have time to be a person. I have time to laugh and have friends over. I have time to learn what it means to be happy.

I am not going to lie to you. When I left, part of me imagined that maybe a nice lawyer or chef would come along, and I'd remarry. But this isn't that kind of story.

When I was trying to sell this book, an editor asked me if I'd been in successful relationships since my divorce. I was caught off guard.

"Yes," I said. "I'm not with anyone now, but all my relationships since have been successful."

No, she insisted. That's not what she means.

I knew what she meant. She wanted a man at the end of my story. And sure, maybe for a time, I did, too. And I wanted it because I wanted happily ever after, and that was the only way I'd ever seen it done.

But in the moment I asked Matthew if being happy was worth it, I was not hoping to swap out one man with another.

I just felt like I was drowning. My friend and I were sitting there with our cups of wine and our grief, staring down the end of our relationships. Both for different reasons. And we were warm with red wine and sun, and our kids were laughing and running in the yard, we all had bellies filled with fried chicken, and my friend had told me that being happy is enough of a reason to burn it all down. And for a moment, I saw that a different story was possible.

On a later playdate, Matthew told me about Ursula K. Le Guin, who took an eighteen-year break between her third Earthsea book and the fourth. This was because she was learning and growing. She had to break down and re-create the patriarchal world she built in the first three books. She had been wrong, Matthew told me. So instead of doubling down, she tried to change the world she created. And I thought about this. And thought about this. And when I'd finally left, I listened to the audiobooks while I walked my dogs. And I learned to find happiness on my own terms. I would learn to rebuild my own world. But in that moment, I did not have dogs. I was sitting on a porch with my friend and a question: Is being happy worth it?

And the answer is absolutely, unequivocally, yes.

Sandra and I have been planning her move for two weeks. Her husband is in surgery, and she needs to move out in one day, while he is in the hospital. It's May 2020 and she doesn't have money for a moving company. I rented a truck and we made a plan to disable the doorbell camera by disconnecting the internet, so he can't watch from his phone in his hospital bed as she moves out. While we are moving, she shows me the pictures of the bruises he left. Shows me the mug he broke throwing it at her head. It missed. But there is a hole in the drywall, and I tell her not to patch it. Leave the hole. Leave the mug. Leave the evidence behind. Don't clean it up. Let him see his destruction. While she packs her clothes and her daughter's toys, I pack up the personal things she has in the closet, her papers, and her books, but I leave his guns. Six months later, she will have a no-contact order. And he will have to surrender his guns to the court.

A few months after the move, I ask her how she is doing. She's a single working mother with sole custody in the pandemic. I expect to hear her frustrations, her worries, her childcare challenges, but she's happy. She's elated. "This is the easy part. The hardest part was getting out."

7

The Revenge Dress

Two days after I asked for a divorce, I had to go to the wedding of my little brother Caleb and his fiancée Michelle. He was twenty-four. So young. Too young. In a phone call with my mother, I told her that Caleb was just a baby. Never mind that he was a grown man and, at six foot seven, taller than any of us. A man in the army. She reminded me I was twenty-two when I got married.

No one in my family knew that my life was falling apart. No one except my brother Zach. Zach and I have always been close, both in age and in friendship. We were born sixteen months apart, and most of our childhood people thought we were twins, with me looking like the boy. So, I told Zach I was getting divorced when I got high for the first time.

Five months before Caleb's wedding, right after I had found the box of my things hidden in the basement, I'd gone alone to Denver for my father's sixtieth birthday. There, six of my father's eight children crammed into my parents' suburban home to celebrate. It was April and the weather plummeted from 60 degrees and sunny to 20 degrees with snow flurries.

It's always hard for all of us children to be back together. We revert to our old patterns, we pick old wounds that have never really healed, our laughter is too loud, the tension palpable. In my family, I am the scold, the do-gooder, the child concerned with getting it right and holding it together. But I was not holding it together. I was not getting it right. And that weekend, I wanted to run into the mountains and scream. But weed had recently become legal in Colorado, so I decided that instead of screaming, I was going to get high.

My plan was a bad one. I decided that under the pretense of going for a run, I'd run to a dispensary and buy weed. But I did absolutely no research. This isn't like me. I am the person who studies the menu three days before going to a new restaurant. I can find your ex-boyfriend's new girlfriend on Instagram in five seconds. These are skills useful for a journalist, but they are also skills honed by an oldest daughter who believes that if you do everything right, if you do all your homework, if you do all the reading, you will get an A, you will succeed.

But I had done everything right and I was failing. And I was failing in the most important way: in my personal life. All I could hear in my mind is *What about your children? What about your sacred vows?* I would hold my marriage together for five more months. But I could feel it ending. And all I knew then was that I wanted to fuck up.

I was thirty-five and goddammit, I just wanted to rebel.

But I was also the mother of two children, both of whom were back in Iowa with their father. So, I needed to screw up, but to do so responsibly. So, my screwup had to be legal and contained. And I needed a Virgil to guide me to the underworld of my breakdown; I needed my brother.

I didn't read the map well. And what I thought was a four-mile run to the dispensary was actually seven miles. When I got there, I didn't have my debit card to get cash. So I called my brother, who had just gotten into town, and told him to take mom's car and come rescue me, because I was not about to run the seven miles back to our parents' house. When he picked me up, I explained my plan. And I knew he was going to hate it, but also, this was the guy who once let me stick lit matches in his ears just for fun.

"Jesus Christ," he said, "you are the biggest dork in the entire world." But he did what I asked; he borrowed our mom's car, picked me up, and we got some gummies. He then took me to a grocery store so we'd have a cover story. And when our mom left to pick up our sister Becky from the airport, we sat on the couch, turned on *Richie Rich,* and ate an edible. It took forty-five minutes before the edible hit, but all of the sudden the world around me felt fuzzy. I lay on the ground and told my brother I felt like I was being rolled up into a carpet.

"What's wrong with you?" he asked.

"I think I am going to end my marriage and leave my husband," I said.

He knew just what to do. He took the sheet cake our mom had bought from Costco out of the fridge.

"Let's just start in on this," he said.

I spent the rest of the weekend lightly fuzzy. I told my

dad I finally understood why he listened to so much Cold-play, and when my mom found out what we were up to, she just put her hands on her hips and said, "Elizabeth!" It was easier to do this than to tell her that I thought my life was falling apart and that I believed everything she'd told me had been a lie. I thought about how rarely I'd been able to fall apart since having children. And I was grateful for the mess. That was April.

By September, I'd asked for a divorce in therapy. The weekend after I asked for the divorce was my little brother Caleb's wedding. My husband wanted to go together and pretend like everything was fine. But I didn't want him there. I'd been sleeping in the guest room since March, and he was not speaking to me directly anymore. Anything we had to say to each other besides "Dinner is in the fridge" or "Please take the toddler to the bathroom" was communicated in therapy or through emails he sent me at night. I woke in the morning to messages that oscillated between apologies and condemnations.

My husband insisted on coming to the wedding. He refused to listen to me tell him how hard it would be for me to fake it. "I cannot pretend to be happy," I told him. "Not in front of my family. Especially not in front of my family with our kids around."

I did not tell my parents. A childhood of being hit with a wooden spoon as a form of discipline meant that I'd learned not to cry; I learned not to show weakness. I learned not to confess the turmoil of my soul. So how could I suddenly and without much notice say to them, "Everything you taught me isn't true. The life you taught me I should want has made me so unhappy. And I want to be happy. I want so desperately to be happy"? And how could I say it the weekend before my little brother—the one I used to rock to sleep when he was a baby—got married to a woman he was so madly in love with? My misery felt like a betrayal not just to my family and my children but to everyone around me.

We went to the wedding together as one happy family. Beyond sneaking away in the car with the kids in the middle of the night and driving to Wichita alone, what choice did I have?

The choice I did have was a choice of what I could wear. A couple of weeks before the wedding, I rented a dress from Rent the Runway. It was a flowing purple dress, with a plunging neckline and side cutouts. It looked good on my misery-toned body.

I'd never worn anything that sexy before. Honestly, I'd never even really tried to be sexy before. Of course, there were the Halloween parties in college where I dressed up in my friend's pleather pants with a cropped Hard Rock of London T-shirt and went as a sexy rock star. (I know, but it was college.)

But I had not ever truly embodied my sexuality. I'd been raised to simultaneously believe both that I was not the pretty one, I was the smart one; and that if I had been pretty, it was a curse. And I got married right out of college.

In the last years of our marriage, I subscribed to a lingerie-of-the-month club, hoping to inspire some creativity in our love life. But the lingerie was cheap and itchy, and I felt uncomfortable performing for someone else's fantasies that always seemed half formed. *What about you but in a necklace and underwear vacuuming?* Okay, I would do that. But what about my own fantasies? But even if he'd asked that question, I had no idea how to answer it.

The last time we had sex was his birthday. We spent the night fighting. And when we finally had sex, I felt empty and shelled out. I was just a body. A flesh bag used for another person's pleasure. After he was done, I sat on the couch and cried. I wouldn't do it again. I wouldn't separate myself from my body just for the enjoyment of someone else.

The purple dress was for me a way of saying that I wanted to be a body. That I wanted pleasure. I wanted to be happy. There had been no affair. No sort of awakening. It just wasn't working. I couldn't hold it all together. So, I put on a sexy purple dress and went to my brother's wedding.

A woman's life can be defined by the clothes she wears. What remains of history's great women, from Hatshepsut to Jackie Kennedy? Clothes and jewelry in museums. Clothes aren't just how we find our place in our lives; they're often all we're remembered for after we die.

Even so, Western culture hates a woman who spends money and time on her clothes and appearance. They mock her for being frivolous. They scold her for narcissism and/or hypocrisy. (Remember Hillary Clinton's pantsuits? The time several national media outlets wrote think pieces on Congresswoman Alexandria Ocasio-Cortez's hair after it was revealed she got a $300 haircut and lowlights at a midrange salon in D.C.?)

But clothes are more than just frivolous accoutrements

to the more serious work of living. In a world where women seldom have the freedom to say what we need to say in the exact right way we need to say it, what we wear and how we wear our clothes can be just as potent as standing up and screaming in a church. For a woman who cannot, for whatever reason, be heard, a piece of clothing can serve as a manifesto. Clothes give women power. Aesthetic communication is one of the most powerful forms of messaging. One that has a long history of imposing oppressive standards, but just as long of a history of breaking those standards. Because in the end, what we wear and how we look have never really been about fashion or beauty but about power. Who gets to look a certain way? Who gets to be desirable? Often the way a woman dresses or presents herself props up systems of power. Yet, when our beauty or our very bodies are "other"— fat, ugly, Black, brown, trans, too small, too large, sexy when we should be modest—we challenge power.

And with my dress, I was trying to send a signal to my husband that I was powerful. That whatever else this flesh was, I owned it. It was mine. I did not want to be just a mother and just a wife, so I purposefully dressed like something else.

And I was completely overdressed for a wedding in Kansas in September, where most of the guests were my brother's army and rugby buddies, an entire family of men he'd built for himself after he left home. They were dressed in slacks and polos. And the women in sundresses. And I was in a floor-length purple gown with side cutouts. I spent the night chasing my children around and avoiding my husband, who had told me I looked nice, to which I responded, "Fuck off."

My mom had taken one look at my outfit and merely

raised her eyebrows. My siblings said nothing. What could they say? I'd always been okay. Aggressively okay. I was not the one who moved back home. I was not the one who asked for money. I was not the one who called our dad at midnight saying I was in jail for drunk and disorderly. All I was doing was wearing an incongruous outfit. But one of my sisters passed me a bag of gummies she'd brought from Colorado. "You look like you need this," she said. I could have hugged her. I felt so seen.

After the reception, my husband and I brought the kids back to the hotel and got them to sleep. With my dress off and my gym shorts on, and the wedding over, I went downstairs to the lobby to get away from the silence and my husband. I don't know what I was expecting to find in the lobby of a Holiday Inn in Wichita, Kansas, but I just knew I couldn't stay in the room. Not with three bodies breathing in the night, wanting so much from me. And me with nothing to give.

I think I wanted to find wine. Instead, what I found was an empty lobby with stale cookies and a TV playing a biography of Princess Diana on CNN. I will always believe that the clerk at the front desk saw the desperation on my face. Because when I grabbed the last two cookies, she went into the back and produced more, saying nothing, just placing them on the plate on the counter. I smiled and grabbed them. I took my cookies to the lobby and watched CNN.

I of course knew the story of Diana, the beautiful ill-fated princess trapped in a loveless marriage, forced to play a part she was ill-suited for, a part no one should be suited for. A woman who dared to value her freedom.

The documentary highlighted the moment that Princess Diana wore the revenge dress: the iconic black velvet low-cut dress with the high slit and chiffon train. She wore it the night that Prince Charles admitted in a national TV broadcast that he'd been unfaithful. Diana was making a public appearance at a party hosted by *Vanity Fair.* The dress had been made for her three years prior, but she hadn't worn it because she had thought it too daring for a princess.

But that night, as the news was all about how her husband, the prince, had been unfaithful with the woman she knew he'd always loved, she wanted to say something else to everyone watching. She wanted to say she was beautiful and powerful, and she would be fine. She wanted to take the narrative back. The dress had been too much for a princess, but it wasn't too much for Diana, the woman. She wanted to take her power back. And she did. The tabloid stories the next day were about Charles, but they were illustrated with images of a stunning Diana in her un-princess-like dress and smiling.

I looked amazing in that purple dress. I was wearing it because I needed to signal that I was breaking. But I'd learned, like so many women, that distress is weakness. So, I clothed my distress in strength. Literal strength. I'd been lifting kettlebells with a friend and going to a boutique gym. I was trying to find a way to begin to take my life back, take my flesh back.

But no, not back. Because to take it back would presume that at any point, I'd been allowed to belong to myself. When had I ever not been wrapped in someone else's expectations?

x x x

I was crying ten minutes into the documentary. If Diana could fight the entire English monarchy to find some happiness for herself, then surely I could divorce a Midwestern engineer? Right? We both had everything we were told to want. She had married a prince. She had two children. She lived in castles. I had not married a prince, but I had married a good man. A man that everyone told me was good. He was a provider. He was a good father. He went to church. He prayed. He saved money. Wasn't that a good man? Wasn't that good enough? He never hit me. Not once. Not even close. He rarely yelled. Maybe he did only once. I was the yeller, the slammer of doors, while he would sit and watch me. Tell me to calm down. So what was my problem? Why couldn't I calm down? And we had children, too. A boy and a girl. We did not live in a castle. But we lived in what appeared to be a charming little house, in a charming little town. And why? Why was this not good enough? Why did I have the audacity to want more? To hope for more? Who was I to think that I was better than this life? This very good life. Who was I to think I would find a better man?

I cried in that Holiday Inn lobby while I watched the story of the princess who burned down the fairy tale. Later, reading a biography of Diana, I'd learn so much more about her depression and her misery. About the coldness of the royal family, about how you could destroy a person with silences. And I would understand, too, why I had needed to leave.

I remember once my mother-in-law, sitting at her kitchen

table, looking at me and my husband, so newly married. "Don't crush her spirit," my mother-in-law said.

My husband grabbed me around the waist and squeezed. "Crush!" he'd said. We laughed. We all laughed. But here I was, eleven years later, crying, eating hotel cookies, and thinking about how crushed my marriage made me feel.

I thought about what Diana had said. How the dress was too daring for a princess. What if in wearing it, she was saying she was no longer a princess? How did that feel for her? Those shoulders so bare? I thought about how it had felt to slip into my own dress. My ribs exposed. My cleavage exposed. I had worn a two-piece bathing suit around my family only once. What were we both screaming with those clothes? Distress? Power? Flesh? And hope? All in one outfit. All without words.

Tressie McMillan Cottom wrote an op-ed for *The New York Times* on the clothes of Senator Kyrsten Sinema, noting, "It is . . . very common in a masculinist strain of intellectualism to consider discussing anything associated with girls and women to be an inferior form of discourse. When we talk about a woman—even in the routine interrogation of how she is able to do her job as a powerful public servant—we are talking about femininity. And femininity does not rate as a substantive form of discussion. This is an easy argument to dismiss because it fails at its own standard: it is unserious." What we wear, for better or worse, so often transcends personal preference and makes a statement. Hillary Clinton's pantsuits. Lady Gaga's dress made of meat. Kim Kardashian wearing Marilyn Monroe's dress to the Met Gala. Each look is as powerful as a press release. For voices sublimated, clothing is a powerful statement. And even for loud voices, clothing can amplify a vision and communicate a message that is hard to put into words.

McMillan Cottom also notes that many modern women dismiss clothing and appearance because good people don't comment on people's bodies, which is a good instinct but often misses the messages and the subtext of our lives. When people don't listen to our voices, our bodies become the way we speak.

There is intentionality when a drag queen performs. They are imitating high femininity in the process of transforming it into a statement on freedom and joy. There is a message when the First Lady of Florida dons a Jackie Kennedy–esque dress for her husband's inauguration. There is a political message when the wife of a senator from Pennsylvania dons a sixty-nine-dollar thrifted dress on her husband's first day in office.

There is also a PR message when Khloé Kardashian debuts a different body shape post-divorce. This is the post-divorce revenge body—a frustrating standard that any newly minted ex-wife runs into. The ideas of both the revenge body and the revenge dress exist in our culture precisely because a woman's identity as a wife and mother is subsumed by the performance of her body. As wives we are flesh for husbands. As mothers we are flesh for children. But as divorced women? What are we?

The revenge body in the revenge dress can be an act of liberation. But it also has a darker side. Performing gender and beauty according to cis, white, thin, heteronormative expectations. Getting a body that makes him regret everything he ever did to you; looking so hot he'll wish he never left: It's still not a body that completely belongs to you. It's still a body performing for a man. The body exists for other people to look at and judge. To see and appraise. Now we are divorced, so back on the dating market we go! When do our bodies ever exist solely for ourselves?

Marriage comes with its own set of body expectations. Partners marry and time passes, children come, age affects us, our bodies look different. Marriage advice of the past urged women to stay looking beautiful for their husbands. Today, this advice is veiled in the language of empowerment: "If you don't feel beautiful and confident, he won't see you that way." But it all amounts to the same—look good or he'll leave you.

The expectation to be good-looking doesn't ease up once a woman is single again. When I was on dating apps, men would ask if I was active. Yes, I was, and I am an active runner. But that's not what they meant. I knew what they were asking: Was I thin? On dates, divorced men would tell me how their partners had let themselves go. How they were glad I was a runner and still working on myself. They said they meant "self-improvement," as if being thin were the only evidence of working on oneself. Once on a second date, a doctor took me on a hike, where he complained about his mother's stroke, which he said she'd brought on herself because she was overweight. When I asked what her life was like, I learned she'd worked as a housekeeper putting him through med school. And she'd refused the personal trainer and nutritionist he'd hired to help her lose weight. When we got back to the trailhead, I hiked myself back to my car, telling him I was off to eat the world's biggest burger.

In her newsletter *Burnt Toast,* author and journalist Virginia Sole-Smith writes about body differences in marriage. She quotes Hilary Kinavey, cofounder of the Center for Body Trust: "To be overly gendered about it: You've got all these women running around healing themselves and their relationship with food. And no one else in their family has to come along?"

Sole-Smith tells the stories of women married to men who are deeply into CrossFit or on extreme diets. "But because our culture socializes women to do most of the labor around food and health, and most of the emotional labor in a family, period, and because this same culture socializes cis men to both avoid that labor and avoid their emotions and equate self-worth with physical prowess—a lot of these guys aren't okay," she writes. "And it is both tough to be married to them and tough to be divorced from them, if you're still co-parenting." What Sole-Smith is highlighting is that many women, who bear the brunt of the food labor, are finding strength and healing outside of a thin-focused culture, while many men are still connecting their self-worth to their bodies. One partner going on an extreme diet or starting an intense fitness program, while the other partner does not participate. This creates an imbalance of bodies and expectations. A husband who doesn't have to experience the ups and downs of pregnancy and breast-feeding, or the daily exhaustion of taking care of small children, might expect his partner to join him in his body makeover, causing a rift. His frustration is supported by our cultural scripts—"She stopped taking care of herself," "She got lazy"—when the reality is, maybe she just had enough and wanted to rest.

But these aren't the only places body image and clothes affect marriage and divorce. During the divorce process, my lawyer advised me on clothes to wear during the mediation. It was important to be neutral. Nice looking and put together. But not too hot. Not too put together. Unthreatening. But not underwhelming. It's the eternal dance—not too fat, not too thin, not too hot, not too ugly. One of my friends who identifies as fat told me that she was worried the judge would perceive her as the less-deserving spouse, since her husband was fit. It's the same difficult dance of women in professional settings, where our bodies are never allowed to just be. Where we are always in the process of negotiating our flesh against the expectations of the room. Only this time the room decides our future.

Diana's revenge dress spoke to me of a woman taking the narrative back in the language she could speak without saying a word—the language of black velvet and flesh. And yet, while it's liberating and celebrated, it's exhausting. A body that thin that tightly squeezed into that dress didn't happen without her eating disorder, her pain, her struggle to control her life. And there I was, too, a thirty-five-year-old woman, on a couch in a lobby of a Holiday Inn, sobbing and eating cookies. Because I had not eaten at the wedding, because I wouldn't eat, I wouldn't show anyone the weakness of my flesh.

I ate the cookies and cried. And the clerk put out more cookies. And I ate those. I ate and cried until the documentary was over. And then I went upstairs and fell asleep on the bed with my two children, leaving my husband the entire bed to himself.

We left the next day. My husband insisted on packing the car, and would forget the dress, and I would incur a $300 charge from Rent the Runway. And later, he'd find my edibles and argue that they were evidence of my instability, my clear mental illness, my unfitness to be a mother. But I wonder if it wasn't instead that the world I lived in was unfit for me? The kind clerk who'd given me cookies mailed the dress back. I indignantly made my husband pay the $300 fee.

And then I posted about the whole ordeal in a private Facebook group with my friends. Except that's what I thought I did. In reality, in my fury, I posted the whole story about me in the dress and the $300 fee as a status update. I realized my error ten minutes later and deleted it. But it was too late; my sister Becky had seen. And I got a text: *Hey, are you okay?*

I called her. I told her I was ending my marriage. And then I called my siblings, one by one. Letting each of them know. In a big family, you have to be quick. They all talk. But they were kind. So very kind. After all, we'd all been through so much. Becky and Cat had almost died in a car accident. Our older sister had gotten divorced years before. We'd been heartbroken and furious and full of sadness and grief and joy. And whatever we had seen, whatever lives we lived, had made us all gentler with one another's pain. Or mostly. When I called my sister Cathy, and told her, very seriously, I was getting a divorce, she laughed. She laughed so hard it sounded like a shriek.

"Finally," she said. "Finally, it's your turn to fuck up. I hope you enjoy it!"

———————

He reaches across the table to grab my arm when he tells me that his wife wouldn't fight for their marriage. They'd been married for ten years and were in therapy because things weren't working. They were fighting all the time. Just little things, like who had to pick up the dog's poop from the backyard, and the dishes. The therapist had asked his wife if she was willing to fight for the relationship. "She said, 'Fighting is such a violent term.'" Their marriage was over six months later. But he wants me to know he was willing to fight. He would have dug deep and entrenched himself. He would have battled. But she just walked away. Ceded the ground. Even now, he still doesn't understand it.

———————

8

Sex After Jesus

I bought my first vibrator off the dusty shelves of a sex-toy shop in Cedar Rapids, Iowa. I tried not to be embarrassed. After all, at thirty-five, I was a grown-ass woman. Anyone could look at me and see the skinny jeans, sneakers, and ruffly blouse and know that I was a Midwestern mother. And as such, it was very likely I'd had sex at some point. Still, I parked around back and hoped no one saw my car. Not too far from the sex shop was the church I had once attended with my ex-husband. An Assembly of God congregation, where pastors preached about the evils of lust, the horrors of porn, the sin of sex outside of marriage—all the new joys I was just discovering. A city of 137,000 people can feel small when you are newly divorced and dating.

The store looked like it was in a perpetual state of going out of business: the fluorescent lights flickering and the gray walls studded with empty shelves. The plastic packaging on the wall of phalluses was dusty, and each vibrator bore a small neon pink sticker with handwritten prices, like a garage sale.

I found the most expensive vibrator—a clear plastic one with a white handle—for forty dollars. I figured it would be fine. Just fine. Sturdy and dependable. Effective. Then I walked up to the counter. The cashier smiled at me. Another woman shuffled in the corner near the lube. She sighed and seemed tired. I drove home. Opened the package. Got to work.

I was raised Evangelical. Taught to believe that sex was a tool for reproduction. To be fruitful and multiply. It was not about our pleasure. In fact, little in life was about pleasure. Pleasure had ended in Eden. Sex, desire: It was all felled by one woman with a single bite from a single fruit. Eve's curse was not only the pain of childbearing; it was also her "desire for her husband." Her desire, her sex, this was the curse.

"Even if you use protection you could get pregnant," my mother told me at age twelve. Desires had consequences. She said she had used birth control for two out of eight of us, and look at where that had gotten her. At fourteen, a girl in our church got pregnant from one night with a boy from the youth group. She had to quit the worship band because her growing belly was evidence of her sin. Nothing happened to the boy. He played football. He went to college. The girl didn't. She graduated high school and got a job.

"All it takes is one time," my mother said.

I had dreams. I had desires. And dreams and desires, for American women, rarely align with sex, and when they do, we are punished for it. So I stayed abstinent until marriage, wearing a ring of Black Hills gold, gifted to me by my father when I turned sixteen, that symbolized my purity. I gave it to my fiancé when we got engaged. I did it as a joke. I hadn't worn it since I was eighteen. I would have had sex, but there had been no offers—not from the two other men I dated before getting married. When I started dating my husband, he was committed to his faith and abstinence. So we didn't.

Some studies show that women who have had no other sexual partners besides their husbands stay married longer. When I was getting married, this statistic was presented as evidence that women should not sleep around. That hookup culture was killing marriage. The study was conducted by the Institute for Family Studies, a conservative organization that exists to promote heterosexual marriage and whose research has come under fire by the Southern Poverty Law Center and Right Wing Watch. Still, their work has been cited uncritically by mainstream news outlets such as *The Atlantic*. The research itself finds that women with the highest rate of divorce have had only two sexual partners. It didn't study the same issue with men, revealing the research's inherent bias against women and their sexuality. But the findings, flawed as they are and used as a cudgel, actually show that free women who know what they are missing are not willing to settle.

Women who have had at least one other sexual partner know what they are missing out on. And they are missing out. In addition to the pay gap and the labor gap, women experience a sexual pleasure gap. A 2009 study found that 91 percent of men climaxed in their last sexual encounter, compared to 64 percent of women. A 2017 study found a similar gap, with 95 percent of straight men climaxing in their last sexual encounter, compared to 65 percent of women. Additionally, while 50 percent or more of women need oral sex to climax, most of them aren't receiving it. Women are twice as likely to go down on their male partners than vice versa.

And a 2019 study found a similar gap among older couples and reported that men are less likely to go down on their partners when the relationship is strained. Meanwhile, women are not as likely to refuse to give oral sex when the relationship is rocky. The researchers wrote in their findings, "Men may think receiving oral sex is not particularly important to women and therefore they would have no motivation to provide it when things were not going well with their partner." It's hard to read this and not feel angry about the way women's pleasure is sidelined and ignored.

This pleasure gap means that generations of women are working hard for men's pleasure, while the men rarely reciprocate.

Because of this, and because of the high social cost of the consequences of sex, women learn early to divorce our expectations and dreams from our relationships. But the pleasure gap, unlike the pay gap, is within our control. We don't need the government to act or pass laws. We can simply refuse. And many women are. More and more women aren't marrying and are dropping out of the dating pool. Columnists and pundits sometimes decry the fact that more men are single and lonely. In response to the news that rates of loneliness were rising, one author, writing in *The New York Times,* encouraged American women to "Have more sex, please!" As if the refusal to date and have sex were somehow a social ill to be solved, rather than a symptom of inequality toward women.

This refusal is happening in the context of a reversal of reproductive rights and a spike in violence toward women. According to *The Washington Post,* "Nearly 1 in 3 high school girls reported in 2021 that they seriously considered suicide—up nearly 60 percent from a decade ago. . . . Almost 15 percent of teen girls said they were forced to have sex, an increase of 27 percent over two years and the first increase since the CDC began tracking it."

This refusal is happening as the wage gap persists. It's happening as one in three men believe that feminism has done more harm than good.

There is nothing about this cultural moment that would make anyone want to simply have more sex. And sex, as a female labor, cannot be the solution to the societal problems of loneliness and alienation. Also, maybe we would have more sex if our partners cared about our pleasure.

I am sure I must have enjoyed married sex at some point. I know there were moments. Intimacies. Small efforts. Some of these things were good. That's the hardest thing to understand about a bad relationship: It has so many good moments. We hold those ragged good scraps, piecing them together, hoping to make a complete thing of it. Something that will cover us, and maybe we can. Maybe some of us can survive long enough that we can forget the bad. But I could not.

For twelve years my sexual identity was, generally, pure sublimation. Eyes closed. Duty to be done. Bent always to someone else's greater plan—God, husband, children. My vagina a conduit. I often found myself in the bathroom afterward, hiding my face in my hands. Exhausted, not wanting to return to the bedroom.

One month after I left, I slept with a man who wasn't my husband. I slept with him so I could never look back. This was the first time for me that sex was a choice rather than an obligation. A hotel. Some whiskey. A cliché that I understood even as I was making it happen. What I didn't expect was to like it. And in liking it to find freedom.

During that time in my life, at work, I was sobbing. And after dark I was fucking. My whole life I'd had sex with only one person, and now I was determined to know men. To feel their hip bones, the divot in their elbows. I wanted to press my palm against their sternum. To feel their heart beating through the pulse in their thighs. I wanted to slip my hand in theirs. To rest my cheek against the soft skin of their waist. From the moment I moved out, on the nights when I didn't have my children, I was doing exactly what I'd been raised not to do: I was sleeping around.

I met men on Tinder, let myself get flirted with in bars. I had younger women explain to me how to seem available. It's all about touching, a woman named Angela told me one night as we chatted. Touch them, just an arm touch or a pat, it's enough. Touch your face, your hair, something. It's enough. So there I was in low-lit bars listening to bleary-eyed bands who were paid in beer, letting a man drunkenly feel me up and noting the experience in my head. I'd jot down notes like an observer watching a television show of a former Evangelical gone wild. Other times, I'd let the voice of a *Dateline* host take over in my head. "She seemed like such a good mother, a good wife . . . then, something snapped."

I wanted to know the fleshy reality of men. So much of my life had been spent twisting and turning myself around them. Moving my body to avoid their arms on airplanes. Stepping aside while they walk down sidewalks, oblivious. Apologizing when they accidentally kicked me in bars or restaurants. In my marriage I slept on the side of the bed I didn't like, curling up to an edge to escape the hot presence of a man. But now I didn't want to avoid them. I wanted to see them, and I wanted them to see me, too. I wanted to stop making myself small, and to take up space, the flesh and fullness of me.

Dating men, studying men, sleeping with men—it felt like lancing the blister. A mixture of pain and release. There was the polyamorous poet. The writer who told me I was overrated and insisted I listen to his vinyl collection. The very nice lawyer. The former white nationalist turned librarian whom I ghosted with no shame. The man who, when faced with a professional accomplishment of mine, told me it wasn't as impressive as his dick. The politician who told me to tell people he had a big dick. (It was average.) The liberal lawyer who got angry when I refused sex with him one morning after he slept over. I was exhausted and wanted coffee first. "But," he whined, "I was looking forward to it." There was the ultramarathon runner who told me whatever I needed for pleasure was my problem. There was the wedding hookup. The married novelist. The date I left after ten minutes in, when he told me if I wanted to be with him, I would need to be a better cook. The sports editor who pulled out his phone and read *Seinfeld* plot summaries to me. I walked out on him, too.

So much of my life had been ruined by men. Men in school who'd hurt me in ways I had long repressed. The writer who'd made me feel so small, hounding me at a conference, insisting I come up to his room. The constant battering of words and judgments and hands from men. And yet, I still wanted them. But I wanted them on new terms—on my terms. The terms of my own body and the terms of my need.

As women we are taught that we need to close ourselves off to survive. A good woman is a woman who doesn't wear low-cut tops, doesn't have sex with men on the first date, doesn't weep in a Jimmy John's drive-thru, doesn't text a chef she dated once to tell him his ramen sucked. We are taught this for our protection. But protection is just another form of control. I didn't want to be controlled. I wanted to be a mess.

And I was.

In 2019, one year after my divorce, I did something people usually do only in their twenties: I went on a romantic road trip with a friend. It felt ridiculous. I was a single mother for Chrissakes. But I went, and the moment we reached his apartment in D.C., he told me he was going to get back together with an ex-girlfriend.

There I was, thirty-five years old, and my heart had been shattered. He said I could sleep on his couch. But I was a grown-up and I'd be damned if I slept on some man's couch and woke up with a sore back. I called a hotel and made arrangements. Got an UberPool and said goodbye. Once I got into the Uber, I began sobbing.

It was nine P.M. I was sitting in the front of the car, and in the back were two very tipsy women, a good decade younger than me. I sobbed silently and felt their stares. The Uber driver was sitting tight-lipped next to me. I felt I needed to apologize for the tears and the mucus and the stifled sobs. "I'm sorry," I said as a way of explanation. "I think my heart got broken. And now I'm a grown woman sobbing in an UberPool."

The women handed me McDonald's napkins from their purses and assured me that this happened. "We've all been there," one said.

"But I'm thirty-five!" I wailed. "And this is the first time I've been here."

Their response was silence. And then one of them said, "Wait, you're thirty-five?"

At the time, their incredulity about my age devastated me. Both for its shock and its honesty. I am sure what they meant was that they saw me as youthful, not at all my age. But what I heard, what those wonderful, supportive, slightly drunk women seemed to be saying to me, was, "How can you still be here with us? Aren't we supposed to evolve beyond this?"

I spent the next couple of days in D.C. in a daze, even though I was also technically there to speak at a college and teach a class of graduate students. But now I was lonely. I felt stupid and humiliated, and I missed my children.

A friend came down from Philadelphia to take me out for drinks at a fancy hotel, and I told her the whole story.

"I can't believe I gave up time with my kids for this foolish trip!" I wailed.

"Just because you're a mother doesn't mean you aren't allowed to be foolish," she told me. Motherhood, age, it doesn't stop us from being needy or fleshy or heartbroken. It doesn't stop us from having desires or unrequited appetites. It doesn't stop us from being ridiculous and human.

So I leaned into the mess, and four months after ending my marriage, and just a couple of weeks after the failed road trip, I turned in my first book manuscript. I wanted to celebrate. In my town, there aren't a lot of clubs. If you want to go out dancing, you either have to line dance at a place called Hazzard County Saloon or go to the gay club called Basix, which is housed in an old McDonald's.

While I do love dancing and have made many mistakes at Hazzard County and Basix is lovely, I also wanted to eat. This poses another problem. Most of the best restaurants in town close by ten or eleven. So if you want to go out and eat and stay out, at some point the night takes you to a bar where after midnight someone is puking in the bathroom and tired bartenders seem to be always throwing someone out. And while, again, I am not above such a night, I really wanted to just wear something nice, eat food, and stay out late.

As it turned out, the local tourism bureau was hosting a Taste of Cedar Rapids, sponsored by the pork council, so I coerced a friend into going with me. I joked that in our small town dominated by factories and engineering, the tastes of Cedar Rapids would be air pollution and chemical waste products. Divorcing in your midthirties means that many of your friends are parents and too tired for this shit. Plus, many of them did their dumb shit in their twenties. But in my twenties I was working full-time, going to grad school, and haggling at garage sales for furniture.

I imagined the *Dateline* episode documenting my eventual murder. Pictures of me sitting with my kids in a pile of leaves would be juxtaposed with pictures of me, drunk in a bar. My shirt too tight, my smile a little crooked. It was pathetic, I knew it. But it felt essential somehow. Like when a character in a movie is forced to go back in time and relive their youth. *Billy Madison* for the slutty mom set. Which is how I ended up very drunk on a Tuesday night, with my mom friend Kristie at Taste of Cedar Rapids.

When Kristie and I arrived we recognized another woman from the neighborhood, who pulled us aside and gave us what we believed to be bubble shots: booze contained in a bubble-like container. We cannot remember. I know, I asked her as a part of research.

"Oh god," Kristie said to me in 2021, "that night. Who can remember?"

Kristie is a vegetarian, so suffice it to say she didn't eat much at the pork council–sponsored event, and neither did I. Eventually, as I was walking from one table to the next, I ran into a man who I had slept with on more than one occasion. This man would later send me pictures of his erection showing through his pants while he was at work. He worked for the schools. I asked him to stop, and he did for nine months before breaking his silence to ask me to help him write a graduate school paper.

Fuck off into the sea, I replied.

Then I blocked him. But that would all come later. At this point, we had slept together twice; it had been unremarkable but easy. I backed up and looked at him.

"I'm here with my girlfriend," he said. I laughed. "Of course you are."

I turned the other way. Coming toward me was yet another person I'd hooked up with. Someone so boring that I didn't want to be stuck in a conversation with him, even as I saw his hand wave toward me.

I turned. Went down another row of tables. I saw a group of people with two pastors from the church that my ex attended. One had just a few weeks prior preached an anti-feminism sermon, arguing that feminism violated God's laws for men and women. The few friends I had who still went there told me all about it.

I turned again, clutching my drink, and headed straight back to Kristie and the safety of our table. I was panicking. Can't an aging mom have a night out without being confronted by every mistake she'd made in town?

I sat down to tell Kristie what had happened. As we talked, she sent a sidelong glance to another table. "Do you know that man, too?" she asked. I looked over. There was my divorce mediator at a table of men in suits. He winked. I slid under the table.

"Get up!" said Kristie, gently kicking me.

"This is where I live now," I said.

She pulled me up, and we retreated to get more drinks.

Later, I would tell my therapist about each moment of that night I could remember. Each humiliation. She told me, "You talk about mess as if it's a bad thing instead of what life is."

And so I continued.

Sex, once liberated from duty, became a pleasure. I had sex again and again. And each time it felt like a revelation. These pieces of me were more than a function of procreation, more than a tool of motherhood or a transaction in a relationship. Each of those nights was a lesson in autonomy, in desire, in asking for what I wanted, and in not accepting less. Because I didn't have to. I could just tell them to go. And I did, if it didn't feel right or they were too aggressive, or not interested in what I wanted or who I was. I owed them nothing. They owed me nothing.

"Goodbye," I'd say. And that's it: I would leave. Once, as I walked out, a man looked at me astonished. "That's it?" he said. "You are gonna go just like that?"

"More like this," I said and slammed the door.

For once, I was in possession of my body. For once, my body had no other function than what I wanted for it. I began working out at a boutique fitness gym. Pushing the limits of what I had been told I could do before as an out-of-shape nerd. I began lifting weights and worked to improve my mile time, until I could run a 5K with per-mile times of just under seven minutes. Because I could. Because my body was mine, at my command. I owed no one the muscle that began to define my arms; I owed no one the desire that filled me at night.

I also learned to define my pleasure outside the confines

of what a man could do. I got that vibrator. Friends sent me links to sex-positive porn. I waited to be destroyed by the lusts of the flesh, like my Evangelical childhood promised, but instead my sins rebuilt me. Now my body was simply my body. Something to enjoy, to explore, to be dealt with, to be loved. Something I could use for my pleasure, my purposes, and no one else's.

In a small purple socialist pamphlet titled *The Power of Women and the Subversion of the Community,* Mariarosa Dalla Costa and Selma James wrote that true female autonomy comes from divorcing our bodies of the expectations of men and capitalism. "Our childhood is preparation for martyrdom," they write. "We are taught to derive happiness from clean sex on whiter than white sheets: to sacrifice sexuality and other creative activity at one and the same time."

I read and reread that pamphlet. Carried it in my purse and read it out loud to women on school playgrounds or at dinner with friends. "You have to radicalize your vagina," I'd say, and they'd laugh, but I wasn't kidding.

A woman who finds joy in sex is a woman to be afraid of because she's liberated from the mediocre machinations of men. One of the reasons the power of the "slut" label still persists is because a woman free to find pleasure her way, outside of the bounds of marriage and the expectations of motherhood and the capitalist requirements of procreation, is a woman who cannot be contained. That's what heterosexual marriage is for so many women: a container, with all the security and limitations that metaphor implies. And leaving that container can feel as liberating as it is disorienting.

When sexuality is divorced from pleasure, it becomes

duty. Reproductive labor. As I write this, the birth rate is declining and think pieces are decrying the loss of a tax base. But more and more women are pointing out that this is a direct result of the political trend toward forced birth. Rolling back access to contraception and to Planned Parenthood, reversing *Roe v. Wade* protections: Coerce birth and women will refuse to participate. Tie sex to reproduction and reproduction only, and the birth rate that you want to see rise will fall. Agency, empowerment, pleasure, and the right to control the outcome of your life, that's what makes the labor of reproduction worth it.

For so many years, I'd sublimated my sexuality. And in that sublimation, I ceded my autonomy. Everything, it seemed, conspired to compel me to do this—the church, marriage, even political powers, which cut off access to healthcare and regulate and criminalize the power of my body and choices. But pleasure, when I found it, was my revolution.

———————

Megan is an accountant. She works with numbers and data.
She likes things she can know for sure. This is the part that
makes her so frustrated because the evidence was there;
she just couldn't face it.

For years, her husband had been sending dick pics to
women—his friends, her friends, coworkers. He told her his
phone was hacked, and she wanted to believe him. Wanted
to believe that she was the crazy one, not him. Because it's
crazy, right? Just to do that? What would possess him? He
was a good man. People liked him, and he was great at sales.

She would ask him about the texts. Once a friend of
hers told her that her husband had sent her an "upsetting
photo." But when Megan confronted him, he had an answer.
He always had a way of telling Megan that she was wrong,
that she didn't understand. He always had an answer. She
trusted him because she'd loved him since they were fifteen.
She tried to fix it with counseling—tried to drown out the
screaming voice inside her. Finally, her sister told her what
he'd texted her.

She trusted her sister. Megan got a divorce, sold the
house, and moved with their children to the mountains. She
says that for so long she listened to him and not herself. Now
she is the only voice she hears—loud, clear, truthful.

———————

9

#NotAllMen

One year after I moved out of my house and my marriage, I wrote an essay for *Glamour* titled "I'm a Great Cook. Now That I'm Divorced, I'm Never Making Dinner for a Man Again." The article outlined how for eleven years I'd cooked meals for my husband and then for our children. I had liked cooking. I loved it even. I thought of food as my offerings of love. But as our marriage dragged on, cooking became less of a joy and more of an obligation. When my marriage ended, I stopped cooking. "I stopped cooking because I wanted to feel as unencumbered as man walking through the door of his home with the expectation that something had been done for him," I wrote. "I wanted to be free of cutting coupons and rolling dough and worrying about dinner times and feeding. I wanted to rest."

When the essay was published in 2018, it immediately went viral. Roxane Gay tweeted the essay asking why women even bothered with men. Rush Limbaugh talked about it on his show. I was a hero: a beleaguered woman who had had enough. Or I was a toxic feminist, making herself the victim. More than one woman tweeted a picture of my face noting that perhaps how I looked was the reason my marriage was ending.

The essay came out as the #MeToo movement was in full swing. Men who had previously been labeled "the good ones" were being revealed to be bad. And not just bad, but predatory. In my group chats and Facebook groups, women wondered who would be next. *Are all men bad?* we wondered. *Does every man have a secret? A rape here, an assault there?*

When I wrote my essay, I was not blaming my husband. I was simply talking about the way something I had loved, cooking, had become a burden. I wanted to talk about how all the ways our gifts of love are turned into expected labors. The trap of romantic love is that it can convince you that your servanthood is a requirement, a necessary sacrifice for the relationship. But, at some point, I had to ask, when was I ever served?

In the deluge of comments on my piece, men took it upon themselves to insist they were good. So many, many men wrote me with protestations of their goodness. They cooked! They cleaned! They were the ones who did it all! I wrote them back with statistics, pointing out that it wasn't about the individual, but about the collective. And according to national data, men did less of this work than women did. Plus, I wanted to know what their wives thought. But it felt like spitting on a fire. The Greek chorus of good men was rising up to drown me out.

After the essay was published, a friend emailed to tell me that she had texted her husband the article with no notes, no commentary. He'd waited three hours before responding, "Is this how you feel?"

"Yes," she replied.

"I am so sorry," he said. "I had no idea." When I read her text message, I cried. That simple act of caring, of listening, of hearing, even for a brief moment, felt so radical and full of love.

By then, I was living in a rented house. I'd moved out from the ramshackle and smelly home we'd tried to renovate for more than a decade into a bungalow one mile away. It had been recently redone and had oak floors and skylights.

When I walked into the house I was struck by how open it was and so bright. I turned to the landlord and said, "I'll take it." I hadn't looked anywhere else, and there isn't much of a rental market in Cedar Rapids, Iowa. But the light was what made me fall in love. The big open windows. The skylights, like two bright blue eyes, looking right at me.

Later, I would learn that the basement would flood. Every time it rained the basement would fill with two inches of water, which poured through windows that hadn't properly been sealed. And the skylights leaked, too. And even though it never smelled of mold, my kids would eventually refer to this house as the mold house.

I hadn't taken much when I moved out. Just what I felt belonged to me. No couches. No chairs. I took the guest room bed, which I had been sleeping on, and the Christmas decorations, but not the tree. Everything else for my new house I bought, or it was donated. My friend gave me boxes of cookware from her single days. I ate off the cheap china I'd inherited from my mother's mother.

I bought a dining room table from a man who made them in his garage using the broken wooden slats from the barn on his property. Everything in that house was something broken reclaimed, something unwanted, something that was going to be tossed away. But in my new space, I felt like it all came together.

I was building a new home. I was still doing the primary labor, but I was freed from the expectation. The thing about kids is they don't care much if dinner is chicken nuggets or a cheese plate, or if the bathrooms are a little dirty, and instead of vacuuming you build a city out of boxes. It was there, in that bright living room, at that table made of broken pieces, that I wrote the essay about no longer cooking. And sold it to *Glamour* for $400. Just enough to cover the cost of the table and a few cheap chairs.

That was the first time I wrote about my divorce. I'd been quiet about it as it was happening. No dramatic public posts. No Facebook relationship change. No enigmatic Instagram posts about growth and doing "hard things." I didn't even delete his presence from my social media. I just made my accounts private. Cried to my friends on the phone. I was trying to be dignified. But then I was suddenly very loud. There on Glamour.com, I'd told the world not just the secrets of my marriage, but all the small dirty details. The ones wives keep so quiet, out of loyalty, out of self-respect, because Gwyneth Paltrow modeled conscious uncoupling, because as Emily Johnson, a self-described divorce guru and the originator of the website Wealthy Single Mommy, told me, "No one likes a whiny divorced lady." But here it was. Nothing dramatic. No affairs. No explosive public fights. Just the slow erosion of a marriage due to the unbearable burden of domestic labor. Labor that held me back.

"It's hard for me to understand when cooking became more repression than liberation, more act of obligation than act of creation," I wrote. "But I knew it then. This thing that had sustained me now felt like a prison. And whose fault was it? It certainly wasn't all my husband's. After all, hadn't I wanted to cook? Hadn't I enjoyed it? Hadn't I found purpose in the texture of the cinnamon rolls, the ache of my arm as I whisked a French silk pie over a double boiler? But who had that ever been for? I couldn't remember."

Years after the story was published, men still contacted me about it. They still emailed or sent me DMs to tell me they cooked, they cleaned, it was that ungrateful bitch they were married to who didn't understand.

And it wasn't just men. Women messaged to tell me that I was unfair to men. "Not all men are like this!" they wrote to me on Twitter and on Facebook and in emails. Or they wrote that they felt sorry for my children and my husband, because I hadn't cared enough about them to keep cooking. They insisted there were so many, many good men. Couldn't I see that? I'd wanted to talk about women's work, but I suddenly found myself in a fight about men's virtue. I was being forced to adjudicate the goodness of the men who messaged me and the husbands of the women who emailed.

But what *is* a good man?

Is it someone who has a job? Someone who is tall? A man who doesn't hit women? Doesn't coerce them into sex? Doesn't slide his hand over a stranger's ass in a bar? Is it someone who is kind? Someone who wipes the counters? Is a good man someone who is good in bed? Who cooks and cleans? Is he patient? Does he vacuum? Will he support his wife's goals and wake up in the middle of the night to feed the baby? The questions are exhausting. And in the face of them I am stymied. Because I don't even know what a good woman is. I don't know what a good person is. I don't think I'm a good person, either. I am not qualified to weigh the scales of humanity. I just wanted some equality, and now I was the arbiter of male goodness. In arguing for my humanity, I became a judge of moral purity. And so many men reached out to tell me not of their sins but their good deeds, as if I were their confessor and they wanted from me a special papal dispensation. A sign from me, a dove from the heavens: "This is a good and faithful man."

They wanted me to say they are the exception to the rules. But I don't know this. I don't know their hearts or their deeds. I don't know the socks they leave on the floor or the sex they refuse to give. But more important, I don't want to be the arbiter of someone's morality. I think of my father saying about my mother how she was so good, the best one out of the two of them. Better than he deserved. And I think of her brittle goodness in the face of their volatile marriage. I do not want this. I do not want a life so rigid and righteous that it has no room for my own failings and humanity. What I wanted was to be as fully human as these men are. Not to push the stone of moral goodness up a hill day after day.

In an essay for *The Yale Review*, novelist Garth Greenwell writes, "'It's not hard not to be terrible' is a sentiment I see floating down my social media feeds with alarming regularity. But I am a novelist because I think it *is* hard not to be terrible. I think it's the work of a life, and most of us fail at it almost all the time. Certainly I do."

Greenwell's essay looks at the messy morality of Philip Roth's *Sabbath's Theater*, and argues for wading into the mess and muck and sex juices of humanity. Argues against our rigid puritanical judgments. And I will think that this is all I have ever wanted, was just to be fully human, which is to say, a meat sack full of nerve endings, failures, and moral ambiguities. I don't want to be good. I want to just be.

One month after my essay was published, a successful businessman asked me out on a date. He was good-looking. He was liberal. He was, at the time, heralded as a local leader. A real hero. Someone on the rise. I agreed to go out with him. I told a friend, and she told me not to do it. "He's horrible," she said. But I went anyway.

On our first date, we met at eight-thirty P.M. on a Wednesday night outside his apartment. Our plan had been to walk to a local restaurant for a drink, but he told me he was going to cook for me instead.

"But I already ate."

"But I am going to cook for you," he insisted. "I had this whole plan. I was going to cook for the woman who won't cook for men."

"It has a poetic touch," I said, "but I'm not hungry. I ate a hamburger an hour ago."

He got angry. "What am I going to do with all the food I bought?"

"I don't know. I didn't ask you to do it."

I felt off balance by his anger. This was a man who was professionally good. Someone who had built a career on being kind and understanding. This was when Donald Trump was still president, and Democratic men were drawing the contrast between themselves and the "pussy grabber."

Everyone had agreed he was good—the local media, the people in town—everyone except my friend. Later there was a whisper network of women who would confide in me about his unwanted advances, his double dealings. Nothing illegal and yet nothing that could be called good. But I didn't know that then. All I knew was that he was yelling at me because I wouldn't eat his salmon at eight-thirty in the evening.

We went on exactly three dates. On the third, he came to watch me do stand-up comedy. Afterward, he told me over a glass of whiskey that I was bad for his brand.

"Why?" I asked. "Because I'm a successful writer?"

"No," he said. "Because you are a single mom."

This was a good man?

Four years after the divorce, I dated another "good man." A midlist writer. He donated to liberal causes, posted on social media about how Black lives matter, fundraised for reproductive rights, and supported mutual aid. But he wouldn't wear a condom. Got angry when I brought it up.

Once, as we sat outside at a restaurant along the Jersey Shore, I ordered shellfish, which came with an aioli.

"This aioli is so good," I said to him. We were in the sun, and I felt like a cat, warm and luxurious.

He looked at me and winced as if I'd embarrassed him in

this, of all places, Atlantic City. "Actually, it's a rémoulade," he said.

I blinked. Then I laughed. I didn't want to ruin the day. The sun. The tequila inside me, making me warm. My bikini top underneath my shirt. My swim bottoms under my jorts. I wanted this to be fun. I was newly vaccinated; so was he. This was the early summer of 2021 when we all hoped for so much, in those golden moments before the most cautious of us retreated once again. But what was happening? Maybe I was misunderstanding his chiding tone. This good man. This smart man. He was smirking at me. It seemed such an unnecessary small stab on a beautiful day.

"But I think it's an aioli." I faltered.

"You wouldn't know. It's rémoulade."

I didn't fight him. I took a sip of my tequila. I thought *Maybe I don't know anything.* I thought *I am just a woman, homeschooled, from Iowa.* So, I smiled. I decided to have fun. Decided I was being ridiculous.

The next night he screamed at me. He screamed because he showed me a movie and I said I didn't like it. He stormed from the hotel room, declaring that I was very basic for not liking this very important moment in cinema. It was ridiculous. I'd always thought maybe my fights with my ex-husband had been because we disagreed politically, but here I was. With a man, a good man, who was telling me I was terrible because I didn't like his movie. When he left, I called a friend who told me to escape.

"You are too old for nonsense, just go, go," she said. So, the next day, on the drive back to New York, I told the man I would be staying the night in a hotel. For a break. Just for one night so I could figure out why we had fought. He pulled over and asked me to get out. Which was how I found myself dumped on a sidewalk furiously googling "hotels in Brooklyn."

I didn't tell many people he did this. This was one of the good men. The men people liked. I worried that once again, I'd be told I am the bad one. *Because look, this is a good, good man. And what did you do to make him turn bad?*

I asked my therapist if I was wrong. What was it in me that made men do this? Even as I said it, I knew I was blaming myself for other people's actions. And yet, perhaps I was difficult. Perhaps spending time with me was like being scrubbed with a Brillo pad. It's something I had to consider.

She blinked and frowned. She'd been divorced twice. "Oh, well, the problem is," she said, "you are dating men."

Women tell me they think about leaving their husbands. Though they don't help out, don't do chores, don't take care of the kids, their husbands are, nevertheless, good men. So they stay. I want to ask them: What does that mean, a good man? Why are they good? Or is it just your love that is making you see them that way?

One of my friends is married to a man who teaches feminism. He never cooks dinner. She does all the work coordinating their kid's many appointments. At one point, she remarks that he doesn't even notice the labor. The feminist scholar.

It was a feminist man who assaulted me. On our first date, I went to his house for a drink before we went out. He pressed me up against a bookshelf and we kissed. Then he pulled my pants down. He wanted to fuck me. I protested, I asked for a condom, but he was strong. Really strong. He said nothing when I said, "No, wait. Please, wait."

And nothing I said stopped him. He was strong. I was afraid. I stayed quiet until it was over. I tried to convince myself I'd wanted it. He was handsome after all. And I did want it, just not like that. We never left his house. After he finished, he went to the bathroom. I dressed. When he came out, he gave me a copy of a book and asked for it back on our next date. I took it. I knew I would never give it back. He'd taken something from me. So it was only fair.

It was a feminist man, a pillar of the local arts community, who pushed me against a wall, with his hand on my throat to tell me I was not worth the money they paid me for my writing. It was this man who called me late at night when I was home with my kids to talk to me about his cock. It was this man who threw bottles at me when I ran away from him.

It was this man who stalked a friend of mine. Who also pushed and shoved her. We eventually learned of each other and became friends. We talked about him sometimes and the wounds he left.

What is a good man?

None of these men have been convicted of crimes. And I know, even now, there are some readers twisting in their minds to forgive these men of their behaviors, their outbursts, their violations. A curse of the social media age is that I can already hear the replies, because they are things I have already heard—I am castigating and condemning a whole group of people based on the actions of a few. "I'm sorry that happened to you," people will say. "It's never happened to me." Or, "He's always been nice to me." Implying that perhaps I am living my life in a way that incites this behavior in men. Maybe if I was calmer, smiled more, contradicted less? Even now, in this line of reasoning, a man's goodness is predicated on a woman's behavior. "He was nice to me" implies my behavior was bad and made him do this, that I am responsible for how he acts. But I've been with so many bad men and never thrown a bottle at them.

At the risk of making you sick of hearing this: Even before a pandemic broke us all open, heterosexual married mothers spent nearly twice as much time on housework and childcare as their partners. And while American mothers are far more likely to work now than in the past, they spend more time caring for their children today than mothers in the 1960s.

A survey of Harvard Business School alumni found that while high-achieving women expect egalitarian marriages, men still expect their careers to take priority. Even if a woman out-earns her husband she still spends more time on chores than him. One study found that women in Australia who out-earn their husbands are thirty-five times more likely to be victims of domestic violence than wives who earn less.

I wrote this book as we entered the third year of a pandemic that was tearing families apart. In May 2020, *The New York Times* released a poll that showed nearly half of men with children under twelve report spending more time on childcare than their spouse—"but just 3 percent of women say their spouse is doing more. Eighty percent of mothers say they spend more time on it." In 2021, labor reports showed that 1.8 million women had dropped out of the workforce. Birth rates are dropping.

The primacy of stable romantic partnerships in our narratives is necessary for maintaining the social order of our American experiment. We need women wedded to their romantic partnerships so much that they'll quit their jobs and abandon their dreams so that men can pursue theirs and someone will be there to raise the kids. In sum, we need women to buy into romantic partnerships so that they will become the social safety net that our leaders and politicians refuse to create.

But when we get these partnerships, all these "best friends" we married don't text us back like our female best friends do. They can't wipe a counter to save their lives. Don't know how to vacuum. And their learned helplessness becomes the punch line to all our jokes. Memes lampoon this male inability to function. A TikTok video shows the face of an exasperated wife on the phone with her husband, who is presumably wandering the grocery store looking for ketchup, and she's lip-syncing to the song from *Hamilton,* "Look at where you are. Look at where you started. The fact that you're alive right now is a miracle." Hilarious. These are the good men.

In 2019, I began dating another very good man, an art professor. I liked his gentle spirit, but six months into the relationship, as the pandemic wore me down, I realized how much care he needed. How I planned meals and dates. How I reminded him to wash the sheets and how I had to ask him

to help with dishes. Small things. But now it was the summer of 2020, and I was a single mother. I had no childcare.
No support beyond the days my kids were with their dad.
And I was working full-time at a local newspaper, where my
duties had doubled. I asked this man if he wanted to go on a
weekend trip to an isolated cabin with me. I could feel myself cracking. I was holding so much together. "Can we just
go away?" I asked.

He equivocated. He wasn't sure. There was so much to
do. His art. He was working on things. I told him I was going
with or without him and if he wanted to come, he needed to
tell me three days before the trip. The date came and went.
I was tempted to badger him. Remind him. But I was also
exhausted. It was one rope I refused to hold. The night before I left, he called me upset. I hadn't reminded him of the
dates of the trip. And he just forgot. Could he still come?

I didn't remind him. *I* didn't remind him? I began to
shout. "You are not my responsibility. You want to come. You
knew the terms!" I broke up with him and hung up the
phone. I was so exhausted and I could not carry the weight
of some grown man's emotions.

That weekend, I took long runs up and down the hills of
Missouri. I drank moonshine around a fire with my cabin
hosts. I decided I would never get married again. I had
thought about it with this artist. I would have married him.
Part of me even believed I would have had another baby. He
seemed so good and gentle. But the world broke apart and I
realized how fragile it all was and how much depended on
the work I would have to do. I realized that even with the
best man I've known I was still scheduling and reminding

and doing the emotional and cognitive labor. And I was no longer interested in doing all of that. I wanted to be the one who was free.

I understand that the life I am trying to live is not about trying to find a happily ever after, but about reimagining what life can look like after you've completely blown happily ever after to smithereens.

I won't get married again, not because I don't believe in partnership, but because I don't want to limit myself to a life centered around a partner. I want to go on trips with friends and my family. I want to force myself to be vulnerable and build a community. And I want to enjoy my own company.

I think of my friends who are queer and the lives they've built that exist outside of the heterosexual norm. Filled with neighborhood gatherings and brunches. I want that.

I am exhausted trying to weigh the balance of a good man. Life is complex and so are humans. I am myself not good all the time. I don't want to walk the tightrope of acceptable female behavior just so a man will one day come alongside. And I don't want my only comfort to be a crown of cold righteousness. I am not interested in being the long-suffering better half. I am not interested in being the corroborating witness of anyone's goodness. I want to be messy and complicated and screw up and try again.

The longer I grapple with this question of "What is a good man?" the more I realize I've gotten it all wrong. I've centered the men in the question. And wasn't that what I was trying to get away from in the first place? In refusing to cook, I was trying to decenter the needs of a man, a fully capable adult man, from being the orbit of my life. And in the conversation, I had to recenter the needs of so many other men who saw themselves in the story, felt uncomfortable, and wanted to push back against the reality of what I was saying. They were, once again, centering themselves, their needs, their emotions.

I am often struck by the contradictions of the data that show men are happy in marriages while women often struggle. If their partner is struggling, wouldn't that make them *not* happy? If marriage costs women more in health and happiness, but men benefit—aren't they actually *not* benefitting? If their happiness rests on the unhappiness of their partner, shouldn't that lead to unhappiness?

bell hooks wrote, "Love is the practice of freedom." And as hooks and so many other radical thinkers such as Frantz Fanon and Angela Davis argue, the freedom of one person should not rest upon the unfreedom of another. The goodness of men should not rest upon the goodness of women.

I do not know what makes a good man. But it's not a question I'm interested in answering anymore. I've been asking the wrong question. The question is not what is a good man. The question is how can we all be allowed to be equally and fully human. We've been making it an individual rather than systemic issue. A "What's wrong with me?" or "I'm a good man" rather than looking at how the structure of heterosexual relationships is oppressive. How we celebrate the martyr mother archetype and denigrate the selfish woman who blows it all up so she can live free. When the men DMed me, I would reply that I wasn't lord god and chief executioner. I was just a human. And I just wanted to be as equally human as they were.

———————

On our second date, I ask him why he got divorced. "The same reason you did," he replies. I have not told him why I divorced.

"Why is that?"

"The marriage was broken and not worth fixing."

Later, when we have sex and he refuses to care about my pleasure, focused only on his own, I'll think I've found my answer.

———————

10

Marriage Is a Joke

The basement where the comedy club is located is dark, and carpet runs halfway up the black walls and pillars. I call them pillars, but they are just basement support poles covered, inexplicably, in carpet. It's one of those places you don't want to imagine with the lights on. Drop ceilings. A U-shaped bar that's backlit with string lighting that could have been lifted from a dorm room.

The whole scene is even more claustrophobic when you realize just seven years ago, this entire basement was under water for several days when the river, just a few blocks away, flooded the town. Most businesses have watermarks on the walls where the water crested. But those are usually twelve to thirteen feet aboveground. This is below, in Penguin's Comedy Club, the only comedy club in Cedar Rapids, Iowa, with an open mic night. And that's why I was there, sitting in the back, clutching my Jim Beam

on the rocks in one hand and my printed-out stand-up set
in the other.

I was a thirty-seven-year-old divorced mother of two
children. I didn't want a comedy career. I was there because
I just wanted to try something new. I wanted to try stand-up
comedy like some people want to skydive. Sure, some people
jump out of planes professionally. But others try it once or
twice for the thrill. I never wanted to jump out of a plane.
But I did want to stand up before a handful of hostile and
half-drunk men in a dank basement bar and make jokes
about my boobs. So, that's where I was.

This was my second time at Penguin's on Wednesday
open mic night. I could only come every other Wednesday
because of my custody schedule. I quickly learned most of
the guys—and it was guys—who came to open mic night
were regulars. And they did want to become famous.

My first night, the crowd was genial if a little ambivalent.
The regulars made me go first because I was the new girl. I'd
signed myself up, and Penguin's is the kind of place where
everyone knows if you are the new girl. So, they put me up
first, and I was better than they thought. And I know that because that's what the emcee, a guy I had once matched with
on Tinder but who had ghosted me, said. "Wow, that was
great! Much better than I thought. You should come back!"

And I did. Two weeks later, I was back. With my notes
and my drink.

Not many women did open mic night in Cedar Rapids.
Sometimes, a drunk middle-aged woman would come. But
she rarely came again. Sometimes a lesbian with a guitar
would come from Iowa City, the more progressive university

town up the road. Cedar Rapids is Iowa City's blue-collar cousin. And a lot of the guys were mostly second shift.

The point is it was mostly men working in jobs they hated, that they'd come to Penguins to make fun of. But I was determined to make them laugh. Because if I could make them laugh, then I wouldn't be the punch line.

I have a great sense of humor. Because I'm used to smiling and laughing at jokes that come at my expense. In high school, the kid who sat behind me in speech class would whisper in my ear about how I was so ugly not even the maggots would want to eat my pussy, and then laugh. Well, didn't I just laugh right along? Out loud, right in his face.

And when the senior in my biology class would shout down the hall about how my parents wouldn't let me date not because they were holy, but because I was too ugly, well, I laughed then, too.

When my dad told jokes about Hillary Clinton and Janet Reno falling out of the ugly tree and hitting every branch on the way down, I laughed, too.

In college, a student sent me an email threatening to "fuck me up" after I wrote a story about his fraternity for the college paper, and then said "That was a joke" when I complained to the dean of students. "Just a joke." I learned to laugh then, too.

Humor rests on incongruities, and in each of the jokes the incongruity—the thing seen as out of line—was mine or another woman's ugliness. We were supposed to be beautiful, to be a sight for male eyes; subvert that and become a punch line. A joke.

I didn't want to be the uptight bitch. The scold. So I learned to laugh and laugh. I learned to laugh because if I

didn't laugh, maybe I would cry. And maybe I would never
stop crying.

Shrewish wives and henpecked husbands are a dominating
motif in comedy. I truly believe the first stand-up set was
Adam looking at God and saying, "This broad you gave me,
amirite?" Stand-up sets often involve men mocking their nag-
ging, fat wives who spend too much money and are always
expecting men to do things like chores. "Take my wife . . .
please!" joked comedian Henny Youngman in the 1930s. The
origin of that joke, Youngman once explained, was that he and
his wife were attending the theater, and he told the usher to
take his wife. The usher thought it was a joke.

"We were happy for years, and then we got married," said
Rodney Dangerfield. He had a whole set of jokes about his
wife refusing to have sex with him. "My wife cut me down to
once a month. . . . This is better than some guys I know; she
cut them off completely."

Heterosexual marriage is at the heart of most classic sit-
coms, full of easy jokes about doofus men and their eternally
exasperated wives, who both hate each other. The jokes normalize the quiet misery of marriage. Every marriage is miserable, the jokes say, so we stay miserable, because that's what
marriage means. When Jerry Seinfeld says, "Marriage is like
a game of chess except the board is flowing water, the pieces
are made of smoke and no move you make will have any effect on the outcome," we're all, theoretically, laughing at the
misery of it all. But eventually the jokes stop being funny.

Wives are always the punch line to the beleaguered male narrative.

My ex used to tell me to get into the kitchen—you know, as a *joke*—but I was always cooking dinner. I was always in the kitchen. And he used to tell me to make him a sandwich, just as a joke, you know, a *joke*. But I did make his lunch, a sandwich, a bag of carrots, chips, and a soda, every day for ten years until our second child was born. And then I couldn't do it anymore. I was too tired. Too depressed. And then he asked me why I didn't make the sandwiches anymore. And so was it really a joke?

Once he got me a mug that said RULE 1: HUSBAND KNOWS BEST. RULE 2: HUSBAND IS ALWAYS RIGHT. RULE 3: REFER TO RULES 1 AND 2. I opened it at Christmas at his mother's house, and his brothers laughed. So did my sister-in-law, and I laughed, too. I laughed the hardest of all. I was always good at taking a joke. Letting it land square on my jaw and come up smiling.

If I laughed, the joke wasn't on me; I could be part of it.

"My wife is a bitch and I hate her," is such an enduring trope of comedy that when comedian John Mulaney joked in his 2018 special *Kid Gorgeous*, "My wife is a bitch and I like her so much. She is a dynamite five-foot Jewish bitch, and she's the best," it drew thunderous applause. Just liking your spouse is shocking enough to draw applause in comedy. Anyway, that wife Mulaney joked about? They're divorced now. And so am I.

Women are supposed to be good at taking jokes. But we aren't supposed to make them. Study after study shows that both sexes say they want someone with a sense of humor. But how that translates into reality is that women want men who make them laugh, and men want women who laugh at their jokes. Researchers have hypothesized that men developed heightened humor skills to get women to sleep with them. But a 2011 University of San Diego study essentially debunks this. Researchers had both men and women submit funny captions for cartoons. Though in a gender-blind test, researchers found that both men and women were equally as funny in coming up with the captions, "humor was more often misremembered 'as having sprung from men's minds,' the researchers write. And, even more telling . . . when the study participants were guessing at authors' gender, unfunny captions were more often misattributed to women and funny captions were more often misattributed to men."

In 2006, researchers at Western University in Canada combed through personal ads and found a gender gap in comedy. Women expect men to make them laugh, and men expect women to laugh at them. Eric R. Bressler of Westfield State College and Sigal Balshine of McMaster University conducted a study where they showed two hundred people photographs of men and women, each paired with either a funny or a fairly straight statement about themselves. They found that women preferred the funnier men, while men showed no preference. Men are allowed to be funny, allowed to make the world the butt of their humor; women are expected to laugh. It's about power.

Humor in women is not often rewarded in relationships. Men don't find humorous women attractive. They don't seek out funny women and don't want to date them. And women learn quickly not to be the stars, but the supporting audience.

Doing stand-up was a chance to take back the narrative. To assert power over a storyline where I was the joke. Divorce was my way of claiming my freedom, but jokes were how I vocalized that freedom. Writing in the 1970s, feminist critic Naomi Weisstein argued that women "must try out forms [of humor] which throw off the shackles of self-ridicule, self-abnegation; we must tap that capacity for outrage, the knowledge of our shared expression." Laughter, jokes, humor are a way for women to regain social control and reduce feelings of powerlessness. Humor also has the potential to rehumanize women. But for me it was more than that: I didn't want to spend my life as the supportive audience. I wanted to be the funny one; I wanted to make people laugh.

It simply wasn't enough to get free. I needed to exercise that freedom in all its forms. And that form was a basement in Cedar Rapids, making jokes about my boobs.

I could not have done stand-up when I was married. Well, maybe I could have, but I would have paid for it in the simmering silences. Or maybe he'd work late and I'd have no one to watch the kids. Or if I got a sitter, I'd hear about how much that night out had cost me. But I was divorced now. And in my empty 50 percent of the fifty-fifty custody, I suddenly had freedom. A freedom I didn't even have in college when I was trying to be good, so very very good.

It had taken months to get here. I was always working, cobbling together freelance jobs so I could pay my bills, and in between, I watched YouTube videos and Netflix specials of stand-up comics. I wrote notes about body language and delivery. How do you hold a mic? What physical comedy could I do? I planned a whole bit about women's fashion where I'd do a high kick at the punch line. I loved a high kick in comedy. I wrote out my tight five, a five-minute monologue of material, and practiced it in front of the mirror in my bedroom. Then I sent the copy to my friend Josh Gondelman, who is a professional comedian. He sent back notes that explained if I talked about robot overlords, be specific. Say Megatron's name. I did and practiced more.

The night finally came. My friend Kelly drove from Wisconsin to watch. We picked out an outfit that was casual yet sexy and would fit my joke about how women's fashion with cutouts and cold shoulders looked like Cinderella's stepsisters had ripped it all to shreds. And then I went on. And it was great.

So, I was back again, and this time, I was on my own. No Kelly. No fanfare. I wanted to do it myself. All by myself.

By the time I went on, I was two whiskeys deep, and about two hundred dick jokes had gone before me.

When I stood up, I began my routine with a bit about being flat-chested and looking like Peter Pan cosplaying as a Duluth wine mom. The guys in the audience laughed. But one guy in the front crossed his arms. He'd gone a few sets before and made a joke about accidentally bringing home a very old woman, he guessed she was forty, and being surprised at how good she was in bed, even though she had wrinkles.

I hated him.

When he crossed his arms, I pointed to him in the small

crowd. "Sir, I have listened to this whole room of men talk about their dicks for the past two hours; you can take one joke about my boobs."

He smiled.

There it was. The power of a joke. The way humor can take back the things taken from you. The way you can turn your weaknesses into laughter. The way you can make people laugh not at you, but with you. I wasn't the punch line. I was making the punch lines. And it occurred to me that these men and I were the same. They felt powerless and disenfranchised by their crummy jobs the same way I felt I did about my own life. They, too, were looking for power. A way to feel special. A way for us to control the world around us for just a few moments. To make everyone laugh. To feel joy. And to channel our rage into happiness.

I went back again and again, polishing my humor, learning to be more physical with my comedy. I had friends look at the shaky cellphone footage and give me feedback. *Lean forward at the punch line. Take charge of the stage. Put your shoulders back. Put your notes down.* Humor was my assignment, and I was going to get an A-plus on that final.

I want to make this clear: I had no ambitions then of becoming a professional comic. I eschew all careers where brushing your hair regularly is a prerequisite. But I have a hard time doing anything halfway. I was all in on this new hobby. This small, dark stage with its dirty Band-Aid-colored wall, this was where I was learning to make people listen.

The regulars knew me but never asked me to join them

for drinks afterward. And that was okay, because so often, I had to get back. I had a two-drink limit because I had to wake up in the morning and take care of kids and pets, and I had to work. At that point, I was working for a literary magazine for $500 a month and ghostwriting op-eds for CEOs, just to make ends meet. I had a contract with a magazine, but they never paid on time. And there was debt from the divorce that hung on my credit like a swiftly growing tumor. On that stage at Penguin's was one of the few places where, for five minutes, I was in control.

Finally, one Wednesday night, four of the regulars asked me to go out with them. They asked me awkwardly, standing in a group and sending over an emissary, who waved to his friends when he said, "Want to come out with us after?" The *us* felt like the collective of white male humor in town, and I was finally in. I had joked myself up to being one of the guys.

By the time I got to the second bar, they were already at the table with their beers. I was the only woman. I ordered a whiskey and settled down. The bar was dark except for the spin of blue and red disco lights. It was karaoke night, and I had put my name on the list the moment I walked in.

I didn't really know any of them. I knew one was a professor. Another worked at a nearby plant, or maybe he was unemployed. I knew only what their jokes were. Depression. Dicks. More dicks. Fucking an old lady.

I started to make polite chatter, until the emissary, the one who'd invited me, waved me silent. "We asked you here because we need to tell you that you need to laugh at our jokes."

"Excuse me?" I said.

"It's just that we all try to laugh at each other's jokes, and you don't always do that. So if you are going to keep doing this, you need to know."

Each man was staring at me. I wondered if they'd discussed this. Was there a group chat? This was a laughter intervention. It seemed as if they felt they were doing a kindness. The tone was one of gentle condescension, not aggression. I would have respected it more if it was aggressive. If they were angry and entitled. Instead, they were polite but still entitled.

I remembered one night when a comedian had been really angry. He made jokes about killing everyone—his mother, his ex-girlfriend—and when no one laughed, he raged, "What's wrong with you humorless fucks?" I was in the back with a friend, who grabbed my arm and pulled me up the stairs and out onto the street.

"It's hard to know," she said, "when men are kidding and when they are serious. I was worried he was going to shoot the place up." We went to a different bar that night. I thought about that moment, with those men staring at me. Was this a joke? Was I a joke? It's hard to know sometimes, what's funny and what's serious. And that, too, is part of power.

"I guess," I said, "that's the difference between us. I work to earn the laughter, and you feel like you are owed it."

I wish I could tell you I left right then. That I picked up my bag and walked triumphantly into the night. I didn't. I had a full glass of whiskey and an open tab at the bar and my name was number seven on the karaoke set list. I had too much invested in the night to leave. And I still wanted them to like me. After all of that, I still wanted to let them know I was cool. That I could handle it.

So I stayed and I smiled. The professor who made jokes about his dick hit on me, but when I came back from the bathroom, I saw him kissing the bartender. "Oh, yeah, that's his girlfriend," one of the other men said.

I got angry then, which is what I should have done in the first place. I don't remember what I said. But I know I said something. Something like, "Why did you hit on me in front of your girlfriend?"

I don't remember his response. And I don't remember mine. Maybe that was the thing. In the end, in those moments, we didn't have words or quips. He had his beer-bleary eyes and I had my whiskey rage. I closed my tab and then my name was called for karaoke. I sang "Goodbye Earl" to a mostly empty bar full of men. They seemed uncomfortable. No one laughed or smiled, or even looked me in the eyes. And that's when I left.

I left because I could. Because I didn't have to be a punch line in someone else's story.

——————

She's furious at me, and she tells me this over coffee. "Not everyone wants to get divorced. My husband left, and I didn't want it. And now I'm lost without him. I wanted a family. I wanted him."

My friend's husband left her for the babysitter around the same time I left my husband for freedom. She's not mad at me exactly. But she's mad I keep talking about freedom. This isn't freedom for her. This was her second marriage, and now it's over.

"Marriage is supposed to be forever," she says. She doesn't know if she can keep the house. She wanted that house. It was so nice and new and full of light.

How can he explain his behavior? How can he justify throwing it all away for the babysitter? The babysitter was married, too. She has three children. I listen to her and hug her and buy her more coffee and a brownie.

My friend remarries within a year of her divorce. She has another new house. And eventually she stops talking to me.

——————

11

The Bachelorette Party

I n May 2021, I went to Charleston, South Carolina, with the person I was dating at the time. We were there to write our books and research. And I was also there to eat barbeque. It was warm and people were getting vaccinated, and I was dating someone, and it felt in that moment like there could be hope.

In the mornings, I went for long runs, then we'd walk to a coffee shop and write and write. We walked around the city, learning about the history of the place. By the late afternoon, all I wanted to do was sit in the sun and wear my floppy hat, the one I'd just purchased, and drink cocktails and people-watch. To be honest, this is what I want to do most of the time, regardless of whether I am in Charleston or not.

One night, as we sat in a bar and drank, we watched groups of bachelor and bachelorette parties from long-delayed weddings wander in and out of the restaurant. They strolled through the streets of the city, teetering on heels, sometimes in matching outfits, trailing balloons and streamers and sashes, performing the last rites of singledom on the bleary-eyed groom- or bride-to-be. The heteronormative rituals of love— wedding showers, bachelorette parties, baby showers—are the delineations between childhood and adulthood. They are markers of social value. What a culture cherishes it cele- brates. And while people can choose to opt out, no one ever has to explain why they opt in.

Charleston is a town that markets itself as the perfect place for weddings and bachelorette parties. It's charming, filled with picturesque backdrops, affordable drinks, churches, and wedding planners. According to the finance site Wallet- Hub, Charleston ranks as one of the top fifty American cities to get married in. And people were here to get married. The world had been upended by a shutdown, by millions of deaths, but the traditions of love carried on.

At night, my date and I watched it all—the bachelorettes, the bachelors, the wedding parties—parade before us through the streets of the city. Me with joy. He with derision. We were both divorced. We both never wanted to marry again.

"Why are they doing this?" he asked, not wanting an an- swer. He had a theory that you could always spot a bachelor- ette or bachelor party by the look of drunken misery on the faces of the attendees. Then he told me about his bachelor party, which he insisted was not miserable. I teased him about the fact that his bachelor party was the only happy one. We are surrounded by bachelor parties. Each bachelor thinks they are happy.

I didn't have a bachelorette party. I was only twenty-two and most of my friends didn't have money. My maid of honor was in vet school, and it never occurred to her to plan something. And it never occurred to me to ask. The entire thing sounded miserable. I didn't really drink much then, and I had and still have no desire to parade around a city with a sash on declaring me a FUTURE MRS. with a necklace of light-up dicks, so I don't know if I would have been happy. Or would I have just convinced myself I was happy because the thing I had been told to want was happening?

So, I sat and drank and watched them, all these beautiful humans, the men in their clean polo shirts and khakis, and the women so beautiful in their crop tops and hair like silk. I watched as they took so many selfies and so many tequila shots, and I wondered if they believed in the story they were telling themselves.

My friend Kelsey told me the story of her wedding shower. Kelsey is the daughter of a Baptist minister in Texas, and the rituals of love and faith shaped her life. But as she sat at her own bridal shower, listening to women make jokes about how miserable marriage was, about how men don't put the seat down or clean up after themselves—all those little jokes that let off just enough steam so the women don't completely explode—Kelsey said, "Marriage doesn't have to be like that."

I think about that all the time. The profound truth of it. How normal it is to joke about the misery of it all. But it doesn't have to be miserable. We don't have to do this. It doesn't have to be this way.

The man I was with was right after all. Everyone did look a little miserable, marching through the obligatory rituals of wearing shirts saying SAME PENIS FOREVER or the hats reading SAME VAGINA FOR THE REST OF YOUR LIFE and taking shots with strangers at the bar. And they would wake up sick and miserable, and telling one another what fun they all had. But here we were, it was 2021. A pandemic had scattered the normal rhythms of life, causing society to rethink the importance of everything from how we grocery shopped to public education. But the moment we were free, everyone reverted to the old patterns.

Here is one version: July 21, in St. Peter, Minnesota. Under a white canopy in the rose garden of my college campus, I walked down the aisle, next to my father, holding a bouquet of pink roses and white hydrangeas. The wind blew the veil around me like a cloud. I laughed and brushed it away from my face as I walked forward. My college roommate was playing "How Sweet It Is (To Be Loved by You)" on the sound system, and I was smiling at my soon-to-be husband. I reached for him and we held hands. We said "I do."

Here is another version: Right before I walked down the aisle, a storm blew through, barely missing St. Peter. The sky was gray and it was hot and humid. I hated my shoes. I couldn't find any I liked for under fifty dollars, so I kicked them off. I walked down the aisle barefoot and sweating. Moments before I'd been crying. My friends I'd hired to do the music forgot to bring a power cord, and a relative had to run to Walmart to buy one.

Days before the wedding, I'd begged my fiancé to just get married in a courthouse, so at least we would have it done. He refused. So, in this moment, the moment where I stood barefoot in the grass and walked down the aisle, I smiled because it would all be over. I wanted it all to be over.

I walked in my dress with the flaw in the fabric underneath, holding the bouquet I'd made the night before because I couldn't afford a florist. I gripped it and walked. The wind blew my veil, the veil I sewed by hand because I wanted it to be a big fluffy cloud, and it was wonderful, and for a moment, just a moment, I remembered the dream. I remembered how it was supposed to be. I remembered that this moment was supposed to be magic. And so I smiled because I thought that if I believed in it enough, if I worked hard enough, I could make that magic appear.

I grabbed his hand. The ceremony began.

For years afterward, my husband's aunts would tell me what a beautiful small wedding it was and people would ask me for tips for weddings on a budget, and I'd tell them my impossible tips: Do all your own flowers, make your own veil, have one bridesmaid, have no extra parties, have your employer pity you and give you food and a tent rental for a discount, use all the money you've saved for a car, live with your soon-to-be in-laws for months before the wedding to save, fit into your wedding dress because you lose weight from stress. Not surprisingly, no one would follow my advice.

Now, I have no wedding advice. I simply say, "It doesn't have to be miserable. It shouldn't be miserable." I wonder how I'd tell the story if it didn't end in divorce. How honest can any story of a marriage be if we still find ourselves loyal to the magic we are trying to believe in?

And vice versa, how true is the story I told you looking at it from inside a bar, where I was with another man, and we were drinking whiskey, while so many people on the brink of marriage swirled around us? And we were in a town where marriage was a marketing tool, before it was a port of enslavement. I wonder if we can ever see the story for what it is while we live it.

The cultural scripts of heterosexual love have no real relevance to the context of our lives. Julia Roberts falls for Richard Gere. Carrie loves Big. Meg Ryan falls for Billy Crystal. No wait, now it's Tom Hanks. Anyway, women are always falling for Tom Hanks. These are the same boring old tropes we all live with and contend with. But we do wrestle and hope because our hearts' reasons feel individual rather than systemic.

And sure, maybe some of our scripts provide for some social context. A wealthy white girl meets a man from the wrong side of town. Maybe he's even Black. But there are always barriers that are overcome. Any social, economic, or political context is there to make the stakes higher, so we know, when these star-crossed lovers dance their way to the altar, that love conquers all. Or is it willful ignorance that conquers all?

These are the narratives we act out day in and day out. They've worn grooves into the paths of our lives. They are so accepted we barely even rethink them. Maybe some pop culture stories try to flip the script, but even if you flip a script, you are still using it. And some people may toss the script out altogether. For the rest of us, in Topeka, the land that Loretta Lynn sang about, one's planning her wedding, one's Saying Yes to the Dress, and one's puking at her bachelorette party.

So many people would rather not see it. Have their wedding at a plantation. Traipse up and down the streets of Charleston, where so many enslaved people died plotting a rebellion, and celebrate their impending nuptials. History layers on itself. Even if you ignore it, you are never free of it. Not ever. Not truly ever.

A couple of months later, in a different city, I broke up with the man I went to Charleston with. The night after we broke up, I had dinner with a friend. Then I drank too much in my hotel room with a former editor of mine. As we downed tequila shots, she told me all about her philosophy of men, which involved shifting them in and out like a baseball team lineup. And then, just as the world began to spin a little faster, I had the brilliant idea to microwave an entire frozen pizza. It didn't work. Laughing and screaming, I ran out of the room with the half-smoking, half-frozen pizza, and dumped it into the trash by the elevator.

There I ran into a woman wearing a FUTURE WIFE sash. She was having her bachelorette party in the room next door. "You look fun," she said. "You should come over."

I held up my hands covered in sauce, which looked like they'd been involved in a murder, and told her no. But I thought she was beautiful, and I hoped she had a wonderful life, no matter what it looked like.

Marriage has formal ceremonies. The wedding. The reception. The honeymoon. Cultures celebrate what we value most—and we do it without thinking. Baby showers, bachelorette parties, bridal showers: To opt out of these things requires more of an explanation than opting in.

Divorce, even though it's an important part of our culture, doesn't have as many ceremonies. There is the signing of the divorce papers. I signed mine on December 18, the day before my birthday. I thought of the image of Nicole Kidman coming out of a courthouse after signing her divorce decree ending her marriage to Tom Cruise. The image shows her in green khaki leggings and a sheer top. Her arms are raised as if she's feeling the air for the first time, her mouth open in a relieved silent cheer. It's a picture of a woman free. Of a woman vindicated. I wanted to re-create that image, but it was December in Iowa.

Instead, the next day, I bought one hundred cupcakes and brought them to the stand-up comedy club. I wore a gold jumpsuit and invited all my friends to come see me tell jokes. Then I gave everyone a cupcake. It was the best kind of celebration.

In Japan, where one in four marriages end in divorce, divorce is still a cultural taboo. But more and more couples are formalizing their splits by having divorce ceremonies. In one ceremony, described in a 2010 CNN article, a divorcing couple smashed their wedding rings with a hammer. The rings, of course, weren't destroyed. But they were damaged. The divorce ceremony coordinator said, "There's no mistaking that divorce is a sad process. But I believe that by declaring your new start in life in front of your friends, relatives and family, you draw a clear line. It helps emotionally."

In the Beidane communities, which are spread out among Morocco, Algeria, Mauritius, Mali, and northern Senegal, divorce parties are a way of welcoming women back to their family homes. It's also a way to signal to potential suitors that the woman is back on the market. In a 2017 story about the Beidane divorce parties for *Vice*, women talk about the warmth and acceptance they feel from the communities during the celebrations. Although divorce may not be an easy or joyous process, the love and care from their communities signal to the women that they are not alone, and that their value does not lie in their relationship status. Divorce is not the end of the world, but the beginning of a whole new one.

Divorce parties have a long history in Western societies. Not because of our enlightened ideas, but because of capitalism. Where there is money, there is an industry ready to rise up and profit from it. But as novel as divorce parties seem, they aren't anything new. In 1902, Mary W. Vitt held a divorce party for herself in Baltimore. The socialite told the paper that the divorce party was the happiest event of her life: "The congratulations of her friends upon her freedom were so sweet that she intends to never shatter the pleasing memory of the 'divorce party' by an assumption of marriage bonds." In 1912, the *San Francisco Chronicle* reported divorce parties were the new trend. The columnist Helen Dare opined, "Times was when the divorcee went into social eclipse with the getting of the decree—waited anxiously, pulling a wire here and there to see how Society would take her, or leave her. . . . But times—and sentiments and social standards have changed. Divorce it seems is one of the social functions to be celebrated."

In 2011, when a dear friend of mine divorced her abusive husband, we got her a cake that read CONGRATULATIONS ON LOSING 158 LBS, and we ate cake and drank wine late into the night. In a 2017 article for *The Guardian*, Christine Gallagher, a professional divorce party planner, said that the first party she planned was for a friend in 2006, and it involved a lot of spicy food and a bonfire. She wanted her friend to feel hot and sexy again. They burned the husband's prize hunting trophy, a taxidermied deer head, in the fire. Other parties had other themes, such as golf, because the husband was cheating on his wife when he said he was golfing; another woman had a funeral to bury her wedding ring. "All of our big life transitions—birth, marriage, death—have a ceremony or ritual," Gallagher noted. "Until recently, there was nothing for divorce. Some people send me hate mail, saying it is in bad taste or hurts the sanctity of marriage. They're entitled to their opinion, but I think the process is healthy. People can feel alone and stigmatised, and there can be a long legal process. A party counterbalances that by allowing you to deal with the emotional side. One night doesn't fix your problems, but it's a big step forward."

Chippendales in Las Vegas, the quickie marriage capital of America, offers divorce party packages. The marketing copy reads, "They say the best way to get over someone is to get under someone else, and who better to get under than a Chippendale? It's not easy to go through a divorce, a heartbreak or breakup for that matter, but when you're ready to click your high heels together and get back out there, we are ready to show you a great time."

The Chippendales website offers divorce party suggestions with some of the kindest celebrations of divorce I've ever seen. Holding together both the heartbreak and the liberation. The site links to a list of one-liners about divorce. ("Divorce is like getting fired from a job you've hated for years!") And links to a Pinterest page for divorce cakes. Thank you, kings.

Of course, these offerings are available because the market is there. Because there are women across America breaking, and they do not want to do so quietly. They want to break and break loud. They want to celebrate themselves and their friendships and their lessons and their lives. They want to laugh through tears. To be messy. They want to be validated and seen, not shoved to the side. They want to toast to the messy fullness of their lives. As the beautiful journalist who listened to me recount how I was old and a single mother and a divorcée said, "Oh, honey, you are just a bitch who has lived." We are bitches who have lived. We have fought for ourselves. And that's something to celebrate.

When I was writing my first book, I interviewed a lot of ministers, and I told one that I was divorcing. She told me that she often offers blessing for divorces and sent me a liturgy of divorce, which read:

Where hearts are broken, grant your healing.
Where trust is eroded, restore good faith.
Where bitterness has taken root, plant seeds of forgiveness.
Do not let anger destroy us,
but teach us to love as you have loved us,
even after marriage ends.

This blessing was a beautiful offering. A way of marking an end and a new beginning. And doing so in the language of religion, which had so often offered me condemnation. The liturgy ended the way many do, but in a way that struck me as full of new meaning in the context of my divorce:

The Lord bless you and keep you.
The Lord be kind and gracious to you.
The Lord look upon you with favor
and give you peace.

Amen.

———————

After the party, she's wine drunk, and we are sitting on the back porch of her beautiful home. We told her husband we were going for a walk.

"Sure, leave! Don't worry about cleaning up," he said brightly. "This is why I pay people, to do all of this. So, sure, walk!"

I am afraid of him. I'm afraid of his forceful sarcasm and his beautiful home. So we do not go for a walk. Instead, we sit on the porch, and she cries. She tells me that she can never leave all this. It's too much.

He comes out to check on us. "You still writing feminist drivel?" he asks and laughs at his own good humor.

"Yes," I say. "There is a huge market for it."

He walks away, and she cries more. I tell her leaving is the hardest part. We sit in silence staring out at her backyard. The pool is covered for the winter, and it looks like a black eye in the middle of the beautiful green lawn.

———————

12

Finding the Night Sky

The year I ended my marriage, I took my two small children on a 1,148-mile road trip from Iowa to Utah to find total darkness. I'd heard a story about darkness on the radio. It was endangered; light pollution from cities had made it hard for people to find. And in losing the darkness we were losing the stars.

I became obsessed with the night that year. I read creation myths about how heaven and earth were once one, only to be torn apart in a violent rending. In a Maori myth, the ripped-apart heavens and earth ask why they have been murdered. In almost every story, life begins in darkness. It's light that must be called into being.

But now light pollution is harming nocturnal ecology—making it easier for predators to find their prey, harder for prey to stay alive. I learned, sitting at night alone in my house, with only the glow of my phone in front of me, that baby sea turtles rely on the light of the horizon to find their way to the ocean, but are easily led astray by the brilliance of the cities that surround the shore. In Florida, millions of baby sea turtles are lured away from the ocean to their death by artificial light.

Light misleads us and ruins the protective cover of the dark. The biggest risk for the ancient sailor was getting lost. Very few ships sailed into the open water. They hugged the shores, the safety of land always in sight. But learning about the stars gave explorers the ability to sail vast oceans. The ancient Minoans left records of using the stars to navigate. Over centuries, Polynesians migrated across the seas. There are no records of how they accomplished this. But people who have re-created their voyages believe they used the sun, the waves, the migration of the birds, and the stars. I start to believe if I see the stars, really see them, I can find my way.

When I was twenty-one, I started having nightmares in which a man was in my house murdering my sisters. When I ran into the street to tell people, no one listened. When I was thirty-three my dreams changed. This time a man's arms were pulling me down into the dark water.

Sometimes it's as if my subconscious thinks I'm an idiot, like I won't understand what it thinks, what it needs. I know we are afraid, I tell it. I just can't do anything about it. When I am told I am drowning, I learn I can do something about it. So I leave my marriage.

When I was seventeen, a youth pastor turned off all the lights in the large gym where we had our Wednesday night gatherings. He'd put black paper over the windows and covered the cracks in the doors. Some of the girls screamed. Boys laughed. But the pastor lit a candle and held it up. "Look," he said. "Even in the pitch-black the light still shines. Darkness cannot overcome the light."

He meant it as a message of hope: that we weary upper-middle-class suburban teenagers should take heart; the struggles we faced would not overcome us. The evil of the world would not prevail. Six months later, the youth pastor disappeared. The rumor was that he had been sleeping with a seventeen-year-old. His wife divorced him.

American society has its own religion of not quitting. Of stick-to-itiveness. Of branding divorcées as selfish. And that religion is the religion of "Do what's best for the children." It's an insidious faith that rests on the fundamental belief that parents (specifically mothers) must sacrifice themselves for their children. In this religion, children are the vengeful gods that must be appeased with our human sacrifice.

Two weeks before I went on the trip with my children, a friend who was miserable in her marriage had coffee with me to talk about how she wants to leave. I listened and gave advice when asked. But at the end of the coffee, as we walked to our cars, she said, "I could never do that to my kids."

Her words hit me like a slap in the face.

"I did it to my kids," I said. I tried to keep my tone even. I knew she didn't mean it to be personal; it's clear she was repeating a line she'd heard before: No matter how miserable you are, you stay married for the kids.

I told her that kids deserve happy parents. "It was hard.

But I believe having happy parents is better than having miserable parents."

She paused. And apologized. But she stayed married.

Telling the kids about the divorce was one of the worst days of my life. We worked out a script in therapy, one that offered up to our children that no one was at fault. That sometimes couples needed to live apart. But my husband didn't stick to the script. He refused. He told them it was my fault. And he cried and they cried. I could not cry, because I had to manage everyone's feelings.

For an entire year, my children would accuse me of ruining their father's life. I would listen to them and hold them and tell them sometimes things had to break to get stronger. And that they were young, and sometimes things just needed time to get better.

Soon their father was engaged, and we had dogs. And I could point to these things and say, "This wasn't possible before. This joy wasn't possible in the old life that you are missing."

In a 2022 article for *Slate,* Scott Coltrane, professor emeritus of sociology and former dean and provost at the University of Oregon, and writer Gail Cornwall break down the flawed studies that for so long warned parents that divorce would hurt their children.

"The 'children will suffer' beat, produced by these different drums, had incredible staying power," they write. "An analysis of popular press articles published from 1968 to

2005 revealed an increasingly negative take on divorce. And the federal government began spending hundreds of millions on the Healthy Marriage Initiative in 2001." Study by study they examine the biases inherent in the "children will suffer" argument and research, and note that children's happiness is a complex mix of factors.

They argue that far more than divorce, it's money and good parenting that lead to good outcomes for children, not a stable marriage. The scientific evidence does not suggest that divorce hurts children, rather that when it comes to divorce and children "divergent narratives could coexist, and the one influenced by sexism, racism, homophobia, and other types of fear prevailed. . . . As a result of the way the Christian right was able to frame—and effectively close—the policy debate, national solutions have focused on individuals' decisions and bolstering the institution of marriage: Choose the right spouse. Go to couples therapy. All but ignored is the government's opportunity and obligation to families. And that disproportionately affects women, Black families, and lower-income kids and caregivers." In sum, it's having access to money and social privilege that determines successful outcomes for children, not divorce.

My children have a stable home, and that is the home I am building. They also have a stable home in the one their father has with his new wife and a little sister. So often the breaking-up of a marriage is seen as instability, but I know that the home we shared was unstable and unhappy. Letting go of the broken wreck allowed me to find my way to safer ground.

Divorce disabused me of the myth that I could protect my kids from the heartbreak of life. All I could do was give them the tools to learn how to handle darkness. All I could do was teach them how to navigate at night through the wreckage of life.

I hoped these lessons would help them see that the world is bigger and brighter and harder and more hopeful than they could imagine. I wanted them to know that they don't have to live in fear. Worlds are ending all the time, big and small. Every day a star dies, a universe collapses. It is both an act of huge loss and an act of nature. I wanted them to know that they could make mistakes and burn down their world and that they could grieve and learn and that it is never too late to fight for their happiness. But all of that would come later. That summer we learned to live in the darkness.

I wanted to find the night sky that summer because I found myself in a place where I was falling into something deep and vast and where I couldn't see, and I needed to know how to navigate by the stars. And I needed to learn with my children.

Artist and activist Amina Ross leads workshops to decolonize the cultural understanding of light and dark, black and white. I took one of her workshops seven months before I went to Utah. How we understand words is how we understand the world, Ross told us. She read us the words of activist and author Adrienne Maree Brown, who wrote that the limits of our imaginations are the limits of our world: "Imagination has people thinking they can go from being poor to millionaire as part of a shared American dream. Imagination turns brown bombers into terrorists and white bombers into mentally ill victims. Imagination gives us borders, gives us superiority, gives us race as an indicator of capability."

During Ross's workshop, we danced around the room to decolonize our sense of space. Then we sat and free-wrote about what our darkness was. For so many people in the room it was their skin, their wombs, their times of rest. I heard "womb" over and over. I thought of my children. I thought of the light pollution in their lives. Literal and figurative. I wondered if a false sense of cheery optimism would mean that they like baby turtles would meet their demise one day in false daylight. Because they could not see the true reflection of the horizon. I decided to take them with me on my trip.

I couldn't afford much that year. I was in debt, working as an editor and ghostwriting op-eds to pay my bills and buy food. Luckily, I had some savings I could dip into for rent. The month of August worried me. I didn't know how I was going to afford school supplies. So, for the first time since my wedding, for the first time in thirteen years, I asked for help from my parents.

I thought *If I can just get there, if I can just see the sky at night, if I can just see the stars, if I can just look into the darkness, then all of this—this loss, this destruction, this wreck of my life, will be okay.* And I wanted my children there. I wanted them to look up with me into the universe, so I could show them that there is beauty here. That what the night sky shows us is just as important and beautiful as anything the sun can.

The year before, just days before I told my husband I wanted a divorce, I woke my kids up and put them in the car. It was August 21, 2017, the day of the great solar eclipse. I'd wanted to take a trip with them, to chase down the beauty of it all with the rest of the country, but my husband didn't want to take the day off of work. "Just see it from our house," he'd said. And so, okay, that's what we were going to do. But that morning it was cloudy, and I started crying. I wanted to see it. And maybe I was exhausted from mangling my life around so many people's needs. Maybe I was tired of never seeing the sun on my own terms. After my husband left for work, I grabbed a bag and started packing. Then I woke my daughter up (my son, the early bird, was already awake), and put them in the car.

"We're going on an adventure," I said and began driving toward Kansas City. We'd chase the sun, I figured. We'd just go and go until we could see light. It was a little deranged. I had a three-year-old and a six-year-old and a couple of diapers and no plan. Madcap adventures don't exactly go well when you have to juggle nap times and Tupperware containers filled with Goldfish.

But I needed this. I was desperate to see this. I could not and would not let one more wonder happen in this world without me. So, I drove and drove. My kids seemed happy in the back with their iPads and snacks. We stopped, and I let them pick out treats from the convenience store. My daughter stared at the candy like they were the crown jewels and she'd just been told she could have whichever tiara she wanted. Except it was better, because it was a Snickers.

I introduced them to two wonders of childhood: the gas station slushie machine and boxes of Nerds candy. Suddenly, I was having fun, too. I realized I didn't have to worry about the budget or someone next to me complaining about the directionlessness of our quest. I didn't even worry about nap time or whether we'd have vegetables. I could let go of what I thought was supposed to be and just let life happen. It was an adventure, after all.

Finally, we stopped in Hannibal, Missouri. We weren't going to make it all the way to Kansas City, but we'd found the sun. I stopped in a restaurant decorated with wagon wheels and ordered a plate of french fries, juice for the kids, and a beer for me. We laughed and made up stories about the sky. I told the kids that the sun was God's eye and today he was going to wink. When the time for the eclipse came, the waitress, the kitchen staff, my children, and I stood in the street with our eclipse glasses (I'd paid too much for them months before). My son insisted on being held. "I just have widdle wegs," he said. I picked him up.

A woman next to me who had come out from a nearby souvenir store patted my arm. "You seem to really enjoy being a mom," she said.

We stared at the sky.

"I do now," I told her.

By the time we'd turned around and got home it was bedtime. After I put the kids to bed, my husband wanted to know what had gotten into me.

"I thought we agreed we didn't need to see it."

"No, you didn't want to see it, and I said okay. But I wanted to see it. So we went."

That day, my kids and I had chased darkness, and I learned how easy it was to leave. One week later, I asked for a divorce.

That next year, it was just me and my kids on a trip across the country. I rented us a yurt in Dead Horse Point State Park, bought cheap food, and packed it in coolers. We mostly ate peanut butter sandwiches. The drive took us three days, and we stayed at the homes of friends and family on the way to save money. I didn't give anyone a warning. I called my sister hours before I arrived.

"I'm sorry," I told her. "I'm a mess right now. I don't know what I am doing, but is it okay if we stay?"

She was raising two children, working full-time and finishing school and living with our parents. She, too, had just gotten divorced. Our parents were on vacation, and she and her kids were in the house alone. She told me I could come. She didn't even make fun of me, and where I come from, that means everything.

In the car, my children and I listened to audiobooks about the Greek gods and goddesses who are pinned forever in the sky. There's Gemini, the twins. One mortal, one immortal. Zeus put them in the sky so they could be together forever. And there's the constellation Centaurus, the centaur named Chiron, who gave up his immortality to free himself of a poisoned arrow and to free Prometheus, who had been chained to a rock for eternity, an eagle eating his liver each day, punishment for giving humans the gift of fire.

At night, as they fell asleep, I read my children star stories from Arapaho myths. There is the story of the splinter-foot girl. A girl born from the splinter lodged in the foot of a hunter. After a lifetime of running from men, she catapults herself into the sky. "I am tired and weary from running," she said.

The rain pelted us in Nebraska, and I had to pull off to the side of the road, because I could not see. The wind and hail jolted the car. The children, on their iPads, asked me why we stopped and I kept my voice cheerful. "Just waiting for the rain to stop!" I said, brightly.

I worried a truck would run into us. I worried we would die. I worried someone would see a woman alone on a trip with two small children and rob and murder us. I worried that I was looking for answers in nature where none would be found. I worried that I was offering up the meaning of my life to a cold and unfeeling universe.

When we arrived in Utah, we set up camp. The yurt was nicer than I thought it would be. I made us cocoa and played Uno with my five-year-old son, while my seven-year-old daughter drew pictures. I took away their screens. I told them they didn't work in the desert. I also told them we were going to stay up that night to see the stars. At dusk, my son pointed to a star and yelled, "Dat's Mars!" I was skeptical and pulled out my phone, equipped with an app to help identify the stars and their constellations. It was Mars. He was right. Later, he would prove to be the child that can always read the stars. The year and month we were there, Mars was closer to Earth than it had been in a long time. When I saw it, I thought of letting go of the comfort of navigating by shores. And casting myself out into open waters. And what new worlds we will find.

The stars came out after that. They were a tangle of light. There were so many of them they seemed more like a web than the pinpricks I saw at home in Iowa. My children were crying from exhaustion and fear that a bear would eat them. I put them to bed and went back outside and lay down on the ground. I didn't need my phone. Because of the darkness, I could finally see the stars, and all of the constellation maps I'd been looking at my whole life and holding up to the sky made sense. Each constellation pulsed out at me, a perfect chiaroscuro. I thought about what it took to make this sky. It took an undoing.

Each star's light tells the story of the past. Because light travels at a finite speed, brighter stars mean fewer years of travel. The fainter ones tell of many years. Light in the universe is a portal to time. The light from a distant galaxy, when it finally reaches us, is a relic of a past we never knew. And maybe I wanted to see the stars because I needed to understand my past before I could see my way forward.

No story I have heard explained what I saw, so I created my own myth, speaking it out loud to my sleeping children every night until it was perfect. Only then did I write it down.

In the beginning, Chaos was pregnant with the possibility of the world. Sick to her stomach, she vomited, and out came Light and Dark. Light and Dark were completely opposite. Light was constant, dependable, productive. Dark was dreamy, full of shadows and stories. Together, Light and Dark had two children, Sun and Moon. One reflective and wise, one bright and full. But soon, Dark grew tired of always hiding around the Light. They fought, and finally Dark left. Separating their lives into Day and Night. The tears of Sun and Moon made the stars.

The next night, I asked my children to tell me their own stories. To make their own myths. Here is what they told me:

The stars are the web of a big mother spider.
The sky is just a sky, and I don't want to see it anymore.
The stars are a million eyes.
The stars are a million lives.
The stars are every single tear that children cry.
The stars are cat farts.
The universe is a God fart.

The night after that, it rained. My daughter believed she called the rain into being. Somehow, in all of our mythmaking, she had begun to believe that she held part of the universe. The part she held was water, and for a whole year, she sat and tried to push away the storms that were scaring her brother. She opened and closed her fists at the edge of pools trying to calm the waves, so they wouldn't splash too hard. I thought about telling her that the universe, even just a piece of it, was not her burden to carry. But I didn't because I also wanted her to believe in her power.

One year later, I took them on another trip. This time to Washington, D.C. They wanted to go. I asked them to dream big, and my daughter said, "Fort McHenry!"

"Baltimore?" I said.

"It's where Francis Scott Key saw the star-spangled banner!" she told me. We compromised on Washington, D.C., with a day trip to Baltimore. And we went because it was a wish that I could make come true.

On the second day of our road trip, we were in Indiana and my stomach hurt. It seized and cramped. And then exploded. I shit in my pants, while driving 70 mph down I-80. I hovered above the seat, swearing and sweating, desperately looking for an exit. I took the first one and sat in traffic at a tollbooth. I couldn't find my wallet, so I was bent over, swiping through the pile of junk in the empty passenger seat.

"Mommy, what's wrong? Mommy?" they both repeated, indignant when I didn't reply. Once we were off the highway and looking for a gas station, I tried to convince them it was fine. "Everything is fine, just shut up, okay? Just shut up." The smell filled the car. *Isn't this parenting? Isn't this what being an adult is? Shitting yourself and trying to make sure everything is okay?*

I found my wallet. We made it to a gas station and I grabbed a change of clothes, then prodded and dragged my kids to the bathroom, until I thought they might cry. In the bathroom, sitting on the toilet, I told them what happened. I told them that I must have eaten something bad at the Cracker Barrel the night before. I told them I pooped my pants. I told them we had to clean the car and that I was throwing my underwear and shorts away. I told them absolutely everything because I was tired of my thin, dry voice saying, "Fine fine fine" over and over. I told them because they deserved to know what the hell had just happened. I told them because we once held hands and peered into the night and saw our salvation. I told them because what else can you say when you are scrubbing shit off your leg in a 7-Eleven bathroom in Indiana besides the truth? I told them because I didn't want to lie anymore.

My daughter was almost angry. "Good thing we didn't eat all that dinner at the restaurant," she said, "even though you kept trying to make us!"

"Wow," said my son, now six. "I guess we all learned a lesson."

"What's that?" I asked. I was expecting something wise. Something grand. Instead he grinned. He had the same wide smile he had as a baby.

"The lesson is no more Cracker Barrel for you!"

I laughed. He laughed. My daughter mimed throwing up.

It wasn't until we were back on the road, still laughing about Cracker Barrel, that I understood we had found our own way.

———————

Laura was happy, she thought. Two kids, a job as a nurse. A husband who worked in sales but came home every evening and made furniture. But then she went in for her mammogram at forty, and there was a lump. Cancer. Surgery.

While she was recovering, he had an affair. He was lonely and said she'd been distant. "No, I wasn't distant. I was in surgery getting my tit removed."

"It wasn't the affair, really," she tells me over the phone. That was forgivable. It was the way he looked at her body now. Suspicious. Wary.

"My whole life I thought an affair was the worst thing that could happen, but I know now there are worse ways to betray someone."

Her body and her husband betrayed her that year. But it's been a decade now. The woman he had an affair with follows her Instagram account. And she thinks about that woman. She hopes she's happy. Her ex remarried although to someone else and had more children. She'd like a relationship, but she's busy with her life and her children and her friends. She teaches yoga now. At fifty she wears crop tops.

Recently, one of her daughters told her, "I don't want to be married, but I do want to be an ex-wife." Laura laughs when she tells me this.

———————

13

Burning the Dress

On July 23, 2020, the day that would have been my fifteenth anniversary, I burned my wedding dress in a chiminea in my friend's backyard in Iowa City. Serena is a wonderful cook and her husband, Adam, a cheerful host, and their beautiful old house is covered with vines and flowers. Separated from family during the pandemic, they became my family—the few people I saw in person that year.

Two years before, Serena helped me report on a story about a woman who divorced an infamous neo-Nazi. Serena had been just outside the room when I interviewed him about his wife's allegations of abuse. She'd bought me a hamburger and calmed me down after he screamed at me. And she was there later, when after the story was published, waves of alt-right trolls would send me photoshopped pictures of me being raped. She was also there when people emailed to say the wife of the neo-Nazi deserved whatever abuse had been given her and how dare I write about it.

The story was published one month after my divorce was final. And for those months afterward, I felt like the world was closing in around me. I couldn't open my phone or my email without a barrage of hate. And for what? For kicking over the rotten log of marriage, patriarchy, and white supremacy. One troll emailed to tell me he'd emailed my ex-husband congratulations on divorcing me. My ex-husband lectured me about my writing and the safety of our children. As if I were the one threatening everything. It cost me everything to be able to write these stories. True stories of marriage. All the ways women are hurt and all the ways they try to get free, even if those women are far from perfect. I told him he could not tell me what to do. I would keep writing.

Three years after my divorce, my wedding dress still hung in my closet. I had never known what to do with that dress. It was cheap and had a small flaw in the fabric under the right arm. I could donate it, but who would want it? I couldn't resell it. It wasn't worth the shipping.

I had always wanted a wedding dress that would look like the one Audrey Hepburn wore in *Funny Face*. In the movie Hepburn plays an intellectual woman who is thought to be awkward and ungainly until a photographer finds her and makes her a famous model. In one scene, she is modeling as a bride in an unadorned bodice with a fluffy, wide, white tea-length skirt. And a fluffy veil. It's an iconic look. The movie is one of my favorites. It's bizarre and joyful and incongruent. But in 2005, tea length was not in style. I was stuck in school in rural southern Minnesota with no car, and no one was offering to take me wedding dress shopping. But I wanted that dress. I don't think I ever thought about another style. I bought the closest version of the dress I could find from a discount bridal website.

The dress was shipped to my future mother-in-law's house. She was supposed to text me when it arrived, so I could immediately look at it and see if it fit, because I had only forty-eight hours to return it. She forgot to tell me. And by the time I got to her house, it had been forty-eight hours already. Upon examining the dress, I noticed a defect in the fabric near the right armpit. I called the company, but they wouldn't return or exchange. It turned into a huge ordeal. I said I'd pay for shipping. And they flat-out refused. Told me their policies were set in stone. I called and emailed and begged. I didn't have a lot of money, and it was my wedding. They told me "Too bad." I reported them to the Better Business Bureau, but it did little good. I was out $200 and all I got was this flawed dress.

I remember sobbing that it was an omen. Of course, I thought everything was an omen. Wedding dresses are symbols, after all, of the purity of the beginning of marriage. That flaw made me feel as if the dress knew more than me.

It was a fine dress, and I looked okay in it. Everyone said I looked good, but they always tell a bride that, even when she looks awful. My mother's friend altered it for me for only fifty dollars. But by the time I wore it, I had lost weight from the stress of wedding planning, and it hung on me. Besides the flaw, I didn't love the dress because it had a small bow on the front by the neckline. I hate tiny bows. I always have. They don't make any sense to me other than to signal "This belongs to a girl, so there is a bow." So rarely do bows add value to an outfit. I used to rip off the small bows on my underwear, leaving holes in the cheap fabric. Now I try to avoid them altogether. But that dress with the bow was as close to my dream as I could possibly have gotten within my budget, so I settled.

It hung in my closet for years after the wedding. And then it came with me when I divorced. A small white cloud hanging over everything. I knew I couldn't even pawn it. Maybe I could send it to Goodwill, but the flaw made it feel cursed. It had been a bargain dress for a cheap wedding. If I sent it to Goodwill, would it become a prop in a play? A Halloween costume for a teen? None of these seemed like worthy afterlives for that dress.

The only possible thing to do with that dress was to burn it.

I had wanted to burn it in the summer of 2019 after the divorce was final, but the busyness of life and a new job and promoting my first book and moving got in the way. When 2020 came around, Serena insisted this was the time. This was the year we cleaned our homes and fumigated, literally and metaphorically. This was the year we burned.

I had been so stressed that year, I hadn't been eating. I'd been working at my local newspaper, and when the shutdown claimed the sports pages, I had, foolishly, suggested in a panicked editorial meeting that we fill the empty pages with a kids section, for all the kids now homeschooling. I was punished for my good idea by being put in charge of making it happen.

I had never managed a print section before, and I had to quickly learn the ins and outs of page design and the politics of the paper. It was a whole second job that was dumped on me in addition to my job as a columnist and a member of the editorial board. I was also single parenting, homeschooling two kids, and launching a second book. At that time, I was waking up at four or five A.M., working before getting my children up, serving them breakfast, and starting school-work. Then shuttling between kids and work until bedtime. After which, I did more work until midnight.

That frantic summer would end with a confluence of events involving a large inland hurricane that would devas-tate my town, political backlash about my columns from the Republican Party, and my objections as an editorial board member to the proposed publication of an op-ed that argued that Black people deserved to be shot by the police. All of this culminated in a charge of insubordination. And then I was fired.

All those storms were still brewing while I burned the dress. They wouldn't break until after. But that July I was stressed. I had constant back pain, and the stress meant I wasn't eating, and so, when it came time to burn the dress, I tried it on and it fit. I was thirty-eight and my boobs were no longer in the same place they had been at twenty-two, so I had to manually hoist them up into position. But the dress fit. I put it on and had a friend take some pictures over Zoom the day I burned it.

The pictures are blurry because I did not know how to turn up the camera resolution. But in them, I'm holding a whiskey bottle and fake smoking a cigarette. I don't normally buy cigarettes, but some had been hidden in a cupboard in my home and I found them when I moved in and kept them, delighted that someone who lived in the house had a secret. I was playing the Chicks' song "Gaslighter" on repeat. "Gaslighter" is a song about Natalie Maines's divorce. "You're sorry, but where's my apology?" Maines sings. A line that hit hard, resonant with so many women especially in 2020, when our society was leaning on us to prop up jobs and childcare, saying, "Sorry" but refusing to offer any form of help. If you are so sorry, then do something about it. If you are so sorry, then change literally anything.

I love the pictures from that day. I look so happy. The blur of the images make it look like I am in motion. In one, I'm leaning toward the camera, an unlit cigarette in my mouth, the Jack Daniel's in my hand, and I'm laughing. In contrast to the clean, sharp, professional pictures of my wedding, in which I am hesitating, unsure, and oh so young, these pictures look like a woman unleashed.

In her novel *Heartburn*, Nora Ephron writes a thinly veiled fictionalized version of her divorce from Carl Bernstein. It's a glorious book. Short and sharp, devastatingly messy, vindictive, weepy, and ends with a pie to the face. What more can you want? It's also narrated by Meryl Streep on audiobook, and I listened to it on many long runs and morose walks while I contemplated my own heartburn.

But there is one moment in the book where Ephron's character muses about the second-wave feminists' fight for equality. These women worked to make their husbands do chores, Ephron observes. And "thousands of husbands agreed to clear the table. They cleared the table. They cleared the table and then looked around as if they deserved a medal. . . . They cleared the table and hoped the whole thing would go away. And it did. The women's movement went away, and so, in many cases, did their wives. Their wives went out into the world, free at last, single again, and discovered the horrible truth: they were sellers in a buyers' market, and that the major concrete achievement of the women's movement in the 1970s was the Dutch treat."

The Dutch treat, if you don't know, is a meal where everyone pays their share of the expenses. What Ephron is saying is that thousands of women left their husbands at historic rates in the 1960s, only to realize that no better men were out there and now they had to pay for their own meals.

I have heard so many versions of this sentiment. "I would leave, but there aren't any better men out there." Or "I would leave but he's the best I've found." As if mediocre partnership is better than nothing at all.

Ephron's analysis is true in some ways. But it also makes me sad, as if the culmination of our achievement as women is only in finding partners.

I see women asking men to do their fair share. And men doing it and then expecting a medal. Expecting never to be asked to do it again. And women, yes, are leaving. Not in droves like they were in the 1960s. But women are leaving and, more poignantly, women are opting out. Women are not marrying at the same rates as they used to. More and more women are choosing not to date. More people are coming out as queer. More and more women are choosing singlehood. And they are realizing that there is something better, and that is themselves, their ambitions and their joys. In fact, they are happy. So much of our culture depicts young girls dreaming about their weddings. But every middle-aged woman I know dreams about living alone in the woods, maybe with a dog.

In 2022, musician Kaya Nova wrote on Twitter, "People think they're competing with other suitors when dating me, but really I'm comparing you to my own solitude. That's the competition. Is your company better than being alone? Am I growing around you like I do when im alone? Do I feel safe? Is there joy??? Is there peace??" Her tweet went viral. Most of the shares were from women saying, "Yes, this. This."

In a 2022 interview with Kevin Hart on his show *Hart to Heart,* actor Tracee Ellis Ross said, "I would love a relationship that makes my life better than it is. I have no interest in just being in a relationship to be in a relationship. I can have a wheel of lovers, do you know what I mean?" She's joking in the last part, her voice dropping lower. But the sentiment is a powerful one. Her comments were made into a video and posted on her Instagram page. The video has over 277,000 likes. In the rest of the interview, Hart pushed back and told Ross that she couldn't find a relationship because she was looking in the wrong places. Implying that if women would only kick over the right rocks, we could scare out the right kind of insects. Ross had no patience for this and redirected the conversation. Ross is a powerful woman. Talented. Successful and beautiful. And even she can't dodge the assumption that being single is some sort of stain.

For as long as there has been marriage, there have been

people rejecting it as a form of societal organization. Many of the early suffragists rejected heterosexual relationships. Alice Paul. Simone de Beauvoir. Shulamith Firestone. bell hooks.

And now, Diane Keaton, who has never been married, dances to Miley Cyrus's song "Flowers" on her Instagram page, and I think of the fierce independence and chutzpah and fight it takes to build the life you want. It takes a radical imagination to see a different way of loving and living outside of the one so well-worn into the landscape of society. We are told we cannot have it all—kids, career, home, and love. Telling us this makes women feel defeated. Makes us give up on trying, on pushing, on asking for more. But we can have it all. So many women have. We just have to find another pathway to get there.

In 2019, I bought a house. I was able to purchase it after my ex cashed me out of our old home. I didn't want what we had. I wanted to build something new. So, after renting for a while, I decided to buy. I live in Iowa, where homes are still affordable. I realize this is a luxury that few people in America are afforded. But it doesn't come without its cost. I love to joke that in Iowa you can buy a house, but there is no one around to hear you scream.

Depending on how you look at it, that could be a downside or an endorsement.

I'd looked for houses all over town. I wanted an older home. I could not let go of the idea of living in a home with history and character. But this time I would choose it. It would have light and no moldy smell. And I would fix it my-self. I often found myself repeating the phrase, "Mrs. Dallo-way said she would fix the home herself."

I found a house, just at the top of my price range. It was a cottage-style home that my kids said looked like a witch's hut, with pointing eaves and wide windows, and it had the most perfect porch. I was in love. But because I was a single woman, the bank was slow in approving my loan. There aren't a lot of people in Cedar Rapids, Iowa, who make the bulk of their money from freelance writing, so it took some persua-sion to convince the bankers that I wasn't just a weirdo. It helped that I had gone to church with the bank representa-tive and, during our discussions, he confided in me about his own marital problems. But by the time the bank approved me for the loan, the house had been sold, and I was bereft.

A few weeks later, the home popped up again on Zillow and I called my realtor and told her to get ready. The day it showed up in my email the selling realtor was having an open house. The market was hot, and I knew there would be a bidding war. I dressed up as nicely as I could without being too intimidating—feminine and fetching, without being too aggressive. I brought a copy of my first book. I was going for the hard sell. I introduced myself as a local writer and made it sound like I was a big deal. I handed him my book. *Oh, just a copy I had. I was going to give it to a friend at brunch, but I have another copy in the car.* I told him I was committed to this town and this community. The previous buyers who had backed out were from "out of state," he said, and didn't want to commit to an older home. I told him I was committed to older homes. I'd been hurt by them before. I'd lived in moldy ones and ones where I had fallen through the floors, but this one, I could tell, this one was worth saving. This one didn't need much work, just some love and attention. Someone who understood what owning that home truly meant.

The hard sell worked. The house had two other bidders. Mine came in at asking price and not a penny above, because I didn't have it. But the sellers went with me. I would like to think it's because they knew I would follow through; they knew I was committed. Or maybe I was just nuts enough to put up with an old home.

My children ended up loving the house. They officially dubbed it the witch's castle and I am the witch. I tell them I will bake them in the oven. They laugh and claim the basement, which they call "Kid Town" and later "Box Fort City." I let them paint on the walls and fill the space with boxes and their own art creations out of blankets and toilet paper tubes and the discarded curtains I took down when we moved in. For six dollars at a garage sale, I bought them a table for the basement, and it came with chairs. I let them paint the table and chairs, and I told them that this house was ours. It was our space to claim and paint and own. My daughter painted a red rose. My son painted a sun and a rain cloud because he said he loved the house and the pets, but we had to get there through divorce. I helped him paint the clouds and told him, "The hard things can lead to good things. Sometimes the only way to get to the good things is through hard things." It made me sad that he had the cloud, but I helped him add little drops of rain. He's allowed to feel his feelings, all of them. My daughter made a sign: BOX FORT CITY, POP. 4. That's two kids and two pets. When our cat Chewy died, my daughter crossed out the 4 and made it 3. When we adopted two dogs, she crossed out the 3 and made it 5.

During the shutdowns of 2020, when they were sent home from school, the basement was their refuge. A world unto themselves. This was their space. This home was theirs. They had agency and freedom here in a way I could never provide had I still been married. Negotiating for the rooms, asking him to put his tools away. Reassuring him that it's just paint and those are just walls and isn't it more important to have kids who are happy than walls that are perfect? I had none of those conversations. We had none of those fights. Because we didn't live together.

The day I moved in, I learned the movers I hired were the same ones who'd moved out the previous owners. "This is hilarious," one of the movers told me. "The hardest part of moving out that family was moving all their guns. The hardest part of moving you in is moving all your books."

I loved that comment. The idea of ownership as transformation. I was making a home. And not building something new but transforming something old. I was clearing out the past, which in this case was literally guns. And in this space, I would be filling it with books and a lot of pets and I would let my children paint on the walls of the basement. And maybe that's the reason I cannot stop loving old homes, because I don't want to change the past; I just want to take what is good from it and leave the rest behind.

And of course, this reminds me of the Bible. After all, you

can take the girl out of the Baptist churches, but you cannot take the Baptist out of the girl. In moving into my old home, I was reminded of verses that talk about refining fire. In 1 Corinthians, the author Paul speaks of how fire burns away pretense.

"Each one's work will become manifest, for the Day will disclose it, because it will be revealed by fire, and the fire will test what sort of work each one has done." The fire here is metaphorical—meaning that life's difficulties reveal the work we've done and if that work is good or not. Owning this home, I will curse out the previous owners for not putting in a sump pump, for bad wiring jobs, and tiling over beautiful hardwood floors, but breaking these things down, taking away what is bad, reveals and redeems so much of what is good. What is worth keeping.

Love and relationships, those are worth keeping. Home and family are worth cherishing. But those things can be accomplished successfully outside of the nuclear unit of husband and wife and two kids. But we need to not be afraid to tear away what's not working. To fight our misery and burn away the pretense. Even if that means walking away and starting something new.

I began this book talking about how the inequality of marriage crushed me. How the years of little labors piled up until I felt as if I was suffocating beneath them. When I divorced, I prepared for the exhausting life of single motherhood. I didn't think it would be better. In fact, I thought it would be harder. No man to help me around the house. No

one to help me with the kids. I'd seen the depictions of harried single mothers and heard the pity in the voices of people
who asked how I was managing all alone.

But what I discovered was the exact opposite. I had
fought so hard for equality in my marriage. I'd pushed for it
and bartered and cried and nagged for it. But what got me
there in the end was court-mandated joint custody and no
longer living with a man.

The first couple of weeks living in the rented house, I
was shocked to discover that instead of my workload increasing, it actually decreased. My ex and I share fifty-fifty custody, so the children weren't in my house all the time. But I
wasn't using that newly freed time on housework; I was using
it to work, often staying up until one A.M., juggling writing
projects. I had two cats. So, theoretically, the workload of
housecleaning and dishes should have been about the same
if not more. But it wasn't. The house was cleaner. The dishes
were always done. There wasn't trash on the floor. That sticky
residue I was always wiping off the counters was gone.

This isn't just anecdotal. According to research done by
the Eunice Kennedy Shriver National Institute of Child
Health and Human Development, single mothers spend less
time on housework and have more free time and sleep more
than their married counterparts. The researchers suggested
that perhaps this is because married women feel compelled
to do more housework with a male spouse around. And that
would indeed echo the findings of Betty Friedan, who noted
that married women seemed to lose themselves in the tiny
labors of housework.

And maybe single mothers are more willing to push back against expectations and let things go. But in my experience, my house was literally just cleaner, because I wasn't constantly cleaning up behind another adult human being. In fact, I've found I've become a little more particular about organization and cleaning, simply because I now have full agency to tidy up the fridge and it stays tidier, and there isn't anyone pointing out how me buying plastic bins to store yogurt in put us over budget. While married, I was more likely to overlook messes and let them sit, simply because they were his messes (for example, the pile of tools in the basement), and any interference on my part was not welcome. Your mileage may vary on these experiences of course, but I am not alone.

I wrote about this experience in 2020, and I heard from so many women who said they'd experienced the same thing. Even if they had sole custody of their children, they felt they had more free time to pursue their hobbies, their house was cleaner, and they didn't feel pressured to do as much domestic labor.

It wasn't all perfect. At the house I rented, I struggled to mow the yard with the janky lawn mower left by the landlord. I spent one afternoon running between Home Depot and calling my dad on the phone, sobbing because I couldn't get the mower started. I had a therapy appointment that day and I showed up to the appointment grass-stained, smelling of gasoline, and crying. "I can't do this," I told my therapist. "I can't mow the lawn. I am not an empowered woman!"

My therapist just looked at me gently and said, "You don't

have to do this alone. You can just ask for help." Her words were a profound recognition that I do not work and live alone. I live in a community of friends, who I can ask for help.

Perhaps the most toxic lie of modern marriage is that it creates a nuclear family unit whole and complete. But it is not whole, it is not complete, and the tasks of life are more than any one family can bear. We need help. We need help at a systemic and personal level. We need paid parental leave, we need affordable childcare, we need childcare tax credits, we need equal pay, and we need a community of friends and family who we can lean on.

I once lamented to my friends in a group chat that I missed dating someone because I missed having someone who was forced to try new restaurants with me, or a standing lunch date to keep me, an extroverted writer, from losing my mind when I've been working alone too long. My friend pointed out that I didn't have that when I was married and that I could just ask friends to fulfill this role for me. What you are looking for is companionship, she told me; you can get that from a good friend.

Rebuilding the ties of community is essential for combating loneliness and not just for divorced women, but for everyone. Author and academic Anne Helen Petersen has written extensively about the need for community and how building it requires humility. "It requires bravery, and vulnerability, and intermittent tolerance for people being annoying, and practice. Like, you just have to keep doing it, and doing it, and eventually it just feels like the thing you do, the people you're near, the community you're a part of. So many people have lost this skill or never had it modeled for them in the first place—and, depending on your identity, you may occupy spaces that are actively hostile to its development. (White bourgeois America is one of those spaces!)"

Community is a practice. And you have to ask for what you need. And keep asking. And if people do not give it to you, you have to find a way to take it. You do not have to settle for the life you were told you should want. You do not have to settle for good enough if good enough requires you to sacrifice your hopes and dreams. You do not have to be a martyr. You can fight for your happiness through whatever means necessary. It will not always involve breaking your life apart. But if it does, you do not have to be afraid. You can Thelma and Louise yourself right off that cliff.

My dear friend Molly is a queer woman, and she moved into a small house in town on a block that is filled with some of her other friends. They call it the gayborhood, and have become one another's families. It's not perfect; nothing is. There are still breakups, divorces, and heartbreak. But it's a model of life and intentional community I admire. My daughter frequently tells me she wants to grow up to be like Molly, living alone but surrounded by her people and her pets.

I don't know what my kids' lives will look like, but I think that at least I've offered them glimpses at new ways of seeing themselves.

I threw a party in the spring of 2022. It had been a long, cold pandemic. But my children were finally vaccinated and I wanted to have people over. I made a vat of spiked cider and filled mugs for my friends. The very same mugs my ex had hidden away in the basement of our home so many years ago. Now they were filled with booze and joy. I tried to match mugs with personalities. The house was full, and people were shouting. Cheese and crackers were stacked in platters on top of the long table that I had paid for with a story I'd written about my divorce.

I thought about how hard I'd worked to get here. To a house filled with friends and wine and happiness. The song "Crowded Table" by the Highwomen is one that always makes me cry; it speaks of community and love and filling our homes. "If it's love that we give," they sing, "it's love that we reap."

"This is going in the book," I told my friends, shouting over the din of conversations. "It's going in the end. Because this is my happily ever after." And maybe it was too earnest, but I thought of all the different kinds of love there are in the world. And I knew that when the party was over someone would help me with the dishes and wiping the counters, and I wouldn't have to ask.

The night I burned the dress, I went to Serena's house, and we sat outside with a handful of other women. I put the dress on over the sundress I was wearing, and they tried to rip it off of me. It was like Cinderella's stepsisters except this time they weren't reclaiming the pieces of my dress in order to destroy me; they were pulling the dress away, trying to free me.

It didn't go easily. But nothing ever really does.

Eventually, Serena took out scissors and we hacked the cheap polyester into bits and shoved it into the chiminea. Serena asked us to cast our intentions for our future, to speak out loud all the things that we hoped for ourselves and our lives. I stuffed the dress into the fire and watched it melt in a potentially toxic brew, and I said out loud that I did not want to find a relationship just for a relationship. What I wanted was love.

But that love was this: people around a fire, laughing and burning. I wanted more dogs and more community. I wanted to fix my house, and I wanted to see my friends. I wanted to create a space where my children felt safe. I wanted them to know they were so loved, that they could do anything in the world without fear because they'd always have a soft place to land and a table where they were welcome. And I also spoke into the smoke about my dreams and my ambitions. I wanted to remove myself from the martyr's pyre and instead sacrifice the roles I had been assigned at birth: mother, wife, daughter. I wanted to see what else I could be.

Acknowledgments

I had to break everything to write this book. And I am so grateful that I did. Thank you to Elon Green, who first came up with the book title and listened to all my fears and told me to be pettier on the page. Thank you to Sarah Weinman for her advice and support and first reads on everything. Thank you to Nicole Cliffe, who helped me find my freedom and who remains my inspiration. Thank you to my agent, Anna Sproul Latimer, who understood this book better than I did. And to Libby Burton, my editor, who believed in my vision from the beginning and whose hard work made this book into a reality. Thank you to my very best friends, Anna Marsh and Kate Johansen. You are my life partners, and I cling to our group chat like a drowning person clings to a life raft. What Kate Said. What Anna Said. Thank you to Brandis McFarland, my hardworking therapist.

Thank you to Josh Gondelman for his friendship and for

being my male sensitivity reader. Thank you to Matthew Salesses for being my single-parent friend during a time of grief. Thank you for telling me that happiness is worth it. Thank you to Dean Bakopolous for his sustaining friendship and good advice. Thank you to Majda Olson for always being right. Thank you to Andy and Carrie Schumacher for creating a place I can laugh, cry, and eat. Thank you to Kerry Howley, whose writing and talent makes me fiercely jealous, but who reminded me more than once that I don't have to be anyone on the page except myself.

Thank you to my city of Cedar Rapids. To all my friends who have been with me on this journey, to the people who fed me tater-tot hot dish after my babies were born, who took me out after my divorce, who celebrate my career milestones with me, who love my children so fiercely and wonderfully. To the people who taught me to hang curtains and gave me furniture and who mowed my lawn and watched my pets. To the coffee shops and bars I wrote in. And the ones where I sit and read alone. Thank you for making me belong. Thank you, Kristie, Molly, Yara, Jessalyn, Katie, Cavan, Beth, Serena, Adam, and Mel. And so many other people who love me and support my writing.

Thank you to every woman who spoke to me about their lives and their divorces. You are a congregation of Liliths, standing outside of Eden, shouting the truth. And thank you to every woman who had the courage to break her life open, to find freedom, and to refuse to lose herself in her marriage.

Thank you, as always, to my children, Ellis and Jude. I hope your world is big, bright, and beautiful.

Notes

1 The End

10 **Research shows that couples** Dina ElBoghdady, "Why Couples Move For a Man's Job, but Not a Woman's," *The Washington Post,* November 28, 2014, accessed April 4, 2023, https://www .washingtonpost.com/news/wonk/wp/2014/11/28/why-couples -move-for-a-mans-job-but-not-a-womans/.

10 **In 2014, a study argued that couples** Ibid.

10 **Eve Rodsky, the author of *Fair Play*** Nicky Champ, "IWD2023: Eve Rodsky on Equality vs. Equity," Transitioning Well, accessed April 4, 2023, https://www.transitioningwell.com .au/eve-rodsky-equality-equity/.

11 **Studies show that when women advance** Maddy Savage, "Why Promoted Women Are More Likely to Divorce," BBC, January 22, 2020, accessed March 20, 2021, https://www.bbc.com/worklife/ article/20200121-why-promoted-women-are-more-likely-to-divorce.

12 **Obama writes that marriage is not a scale** Michelle Obama, *The Light We Carry* (New York: Crown, 2022).

12 **Charlotte Ljung, a Swedish CEO of a bed** Savage, "Why Promoted Women."

15 **"even in times of greatest distress"** Milan Kundera, *The Unbearable Lightness of Being* (New York: Harper & Row, 1984).

16 **"More good women have been lost to marriage"** *101 Dalmatians,* directed by Stephen Herek (Walt Disney Pictures, 1996).

17 **"Before all else you are a wife"** Henrik Ibsen and Nicholas Rudall, *A Doll's House* (Chicago: I. R. Dee, 1999).

17 **But the moment the war was over** Sally Herships and Darian Woods, "That Time America Paid for Universal Day Care," NPR, June 30, 2021, accessed December 10, 2022, https://www.npr.org/2021/06/30/1011968802/that-time-america-paid-for-universal-daycare#:.

19 **Nearly 70 percent of divorces** "Women More Likely Than Men to Initiate Divorces, but Not Non-Marital Breakups," American Sociological Association, August 22, 2015, accessed April 4, 2023, https://www.asanet.org/women-more-likely-men-initiate-divorces-not-non-marital-breakups/?hilite=initiate+divorce.

24 **The divorce rate in America currently** Francesca Marino, "Divorce Rate in the U.S.: Geographic Variation, 2021," *Family Profiles,* FP-22-26, National Center for Family and Marriage Research, accessed April 4, 2023, https://doi.org/10.25035/ncfmr/fp-22-26.

24 **And fewer and fewer Americans** Kim Parker and Renee Stepler, "As U.S. Marriage Rate Hovers at 50%, Education Gap in Marital Status Widens," Pew Research Center, September 14, 2017, accessed April 4, 2023, http://pewrsr.ch/2eYAuZM.

24 **Dinah Hannaford, associate professor** Kristin Rogers, "Why Women Do or Don't Change Their Name When They Get Married," CNN, July 19, 2022, accessed April 4, 2023, https://edition.cnn.com/2022/07/19/health/last-name-change-marriage-reasons-wellness/index.htm.

2 Just a Girl in a Country Song

35 **It offended men and was banned** Mary Bufwack, "Kitty Wells: Don't Blame the 'Honky-Tonk,'" NPR, December 14, 2008, https://www.npr.org/2008/12/14/98201349/kitty-wells-dont-blame-the-honky-tonk.

35 **was the first number one *Billboard*** Ibid.

36 **"It was a delicate balance"** "Marissa Moss," interview by Lyz Lenz, *Interview,* August 26, 2021.

37 **In 2000, the number of women** "Labor Force Participation Rate–Women," Federal Reserve Economic Source, accessed April 4, 2023, https://fred.stlouisfed.org/series/LNS11300002.

37   **It's not that America was** Bryce Covert, "The Best Era for
     Working Women Was 20 Years Ago," *The New York Times,* Sep-
     tember 2, 2017, accessed April 5, 2023, https://www.nytimes
     .com/2017/09/02/opinion/sunday/working-women-decline-1990s
     .html.

38   **America, once a leader in gender** "Gender Wage Gap,"
     OECD, accessed April 5, 2023, https://data.oecd.org/earnwage/
     gender-wage-gap.htm.

41   **A tweet by Lucy Huber** Lucy Huber (@clhubes), "Why is male
     country music like," Twitter, June 8, 2021, 11:09 A.M., https://
     twitter.com/clhubes/status/1402296687423635463?lang=en.

41   **In a podcast, Dolly Parton** Jad Abumrad, "Dollitics," *Dolly Par-
     ton's America,* produced and reported by Shima Oliaee, podcast,
     WNYC Studios, 2019, https://www.wnycstudios.org/podcasts/
     dolly-partons-america.

3   Down the Aisle

49   **Before societies understood the concept** Hannah Booth,
     "The Kingdom of Women: The Society Where a Man Is Never
     the Boss," *The Guardian,* April 1, 2017, accessed April 4, 2023,
     https://www.theguardian.com/lifeandstyle/2017/apr/01/the
     -kingdom-of-women-the-tibetan-tribe-where-a-man-is-never-the
     -boss.

50   **most societies have some form of marriage** Carol R. Em-
     ber, Benjamin Gonzalez, and Daniel McClosky, "Marriage and
     Family," HRAF, July 16, 2021, accessed April 5, 2023, https://
     hraf.yale.edu/ehc/summaries/marriage-and-family#universality-of
     -marriage.

50   **Divorce rates are hard to calculate** Christie Bieber, "Reveal-
     ing Divorce Statistics in 2023," *Forbes,* May 4, 2023, https://www
     .forbes.com/advisor/legal/divorce/divorce-statistics/.

50   **In 2014, Claire Cain Miller** Bella DePaulo, "What Is the
     Divorce Rate, Really?," *Psychology Today,* February 2, 2017, https://
     www.psychologytoday.com/us/blog/living-single/201702/what-is
     -the-divorce-rate-really.

51   **"About 75 percent of societies"** Ibid.

51   **Anthropologists speculate that the custom** Ibid.

51   **The Guarani of South America** Ibid.

52   **Even today, more than 50 percent** Esteban Ortiz-Ospina

and Max Roser, "Marriages and Divorces," Our World in Data, accessed April 9, 2023, https://ourworldindata.org/marriages-and-divorces.

54   **"the one is the husband"** William Blackstone, *Commentaries on the Laws of England* (Oxford: Clarendon Press, 1765).

54   **"The common law tradition"** Renata Grossi, *Looking for Love in the Legal Discourse of Marriage* (Canberra: Australian National University, 2014).

54   **She became the patron saint** Jade King, *Saint Wilgefortis: A Bearded Woman with a Queer History,* August 13, 2021, accessed April 4, 2023, https://artuk.org/discover/stories/saint-wilgefortis-a-bearded-woman-with-a-queer-history#.

54   **Some art historians theorize** Ibid.

56   **And women are more likely to be murdered** "The Scope of the Problem: Intimate Partner Homicide Statistics," VAWnet, accessed April 4, 2023, https://vawnet.org/sc/scope-problem-intimate-partner-homicide-statistics.

59   **getting a divorce required an act of Parliament** Amanda Foreman, "The Heartbreaking History of Divorce," *Smithsonian Magazine,* February 2014, https://www.smithsonianmag.com/history/heartbreaking-history-of-divorce-180949439/.

59   **Pilgrims granted at least nine divorces** Glenda Riley, *Divorce: An American Tradition* (Omaha: University of Nebraska Press, 1997).

59   **divorce was easier to attain in the new country** Michel Chevalier, *Society, Manners, and Politics in the United States* (Boston: Weeks, Jordan, and Company, 1839).

60   **"Cruel to continue by violence"** Frank L. Dewey, "Thomas Jefferson's Notes on Divorce," *The William and Mary Quarterly* 39, no. 1 (1982): 212–23.

60   **Overwhelmed by the number of divorce** Richard H. Chused, *Private Acts in Public Spaces: A Social History of Divorce in the Formative Era of American Family Law* (Philadelphia: University of Pennsylvania Press, 1994).

61   **The reasons for many of these early divorces** Riley, *Divorce.*

61   **"I do hereby forewarn"** Bill Carey, "Runaway Wives in Tennessee's Antebellum Era," *The Tennessee Magazine,* March 1, 2018, https://www.tnmagazine.org/runaway-wives-tennessees-antebellum-era/.

61 **In the 1800s, the Midwestern states** April White, *The Divorce Colonies* (New York: Hachette, 2022).

62 **Freedom was what so many** Ibid.

63 **That same year, American suffragists** "Declaration of Sentiments," National Park Service, 1848, accessed April 5, 2023, https://www.nps.gov/wori/learn/historyculture/declaration-of-sentiments.htm.

64 **The book *Far More Terrible*** Patrick N. Minges, *Far More Terrible for Women: Personal Accounts of Women in Slavery* (Winston-Salem, N.C.: Blair, 2006).

65 **"Black women's unfreedom"** Aneeka A. Henderson, *Veil and Vow: Marriage Matters in Contemporary African American Culture* (Chapel Hill: University of North Carolina Press, 2020).

65 **"a free, unregulated, and equitable romance market"** Ibid.

65 **Black women are more likely to be single** Anna Brown, "A Profile of Single Americans," Pew Research Center, August 20, 2020, accessed April 9, 2023, https://www.pewresearch.org/social-trends/2020/08/20/a-profile-of-single-americans/.

65 **least desirable dating cohort** Christian Rudder, "Race and Attraction," OkTrends, September 10, 2014, accessed April 9, 2023, https://gwern.net/doc/psychology/okcupid/raceandattraction20092014.html.

66 **"a program for the privileged"** Michael Warner, *The Trouble with Normal: Sex, Politics, and the Ethics of Queer Life* (New York: Free Press, 1999).

66 **Today, nearly half of all Black women** Chanell Washington and Laquitta Walker, "District of Columbia Had Lowest Percentage of Married Black Adults in 2015–2019," U.S. Census Bureau, July 19, 2022, accessed April 5, 2023, https://www.census.gov/content/census/en/library/stories/2022/07/marriage-prevalence-for-black-adults-varies-by-state.html/.

66 **In the Queer Manifesto** "Queer Nation Manifesto: A Manifesto Written in 1990 by ACT UP," Verso Books, June 29, 2021, accessed April 4, 2023, https://www.versobooks.com/blogs/news/5106-queer-nation-manifesto-queers-read-this?fbclid=IwAR2KyTxVE2fszez34b2AAGGEoD-lM7IIaCML4edp9hG6aGumZsWrz7pIsFU.

67 **"The pandemic has only deepened"** Minda Honey, "Single Black Women and the Lies About Our Love Lives," Andscape,

February 14, 2022, accessed April 4, 2023, https://andscape.com/features/single-black-women-and-the-lies-about-our-love-lives/.

68 **Historian Randal Olson** Randal S. Olson, "144 Years of Marriage and Divorce in 1 Chart," June 15, 2015, accessed April 4, 2023, https://randalolson.com/2015/06/15/144-years-of-marriage-and-divorce-in-1-chart/.

69 **Historians attribute the leap** Ana Swanson, "144 Years of Marriage and Divorce in the United States, in One Chart," *The Washington Post,* June 23, 2015, accessed April 5, 2023, https://www.washingtonpost.com/news/wonk/wp/2015/06/23/144-years-of-marriage-and-divorce-in-the-united-states-in-one-chart/.

69 **In 1987, researcher Shere Hite** Emily Langer, "Shere Hite, Author of Taboo-Breaking 'Hite Reports' on Human Sexuality, Dies at 77," *The Washington Post,* September 11, 2020, accessed April 4, 2023, https://www.washingtonpost.com/local/obituaries/shere-hite-author-of-taboo-busting-hite-reports-on-human-sexuality-dies-at-77/2020/09/11/0c60e96e-f397-11ea-b796-2dd09962649c_story.html.

70 **men have benefited from the institution** Susan Faludi, *Backlash: The Undeclared War Against Women* (New York: Crown, 1991).

70 **"There are few findings more consistent"** Ibid.

70 **Meanwhile, women are far less likely** Kim Parker and Renee Stepler, "As U.S. Marriage Rate Hovers at 50%, Education Gap in Marital Status Widens," Pew Research Center, September 14, 2017, accessed April 4, 2023, http://pewrsr.ch/2eYAuZM.

71 **60 percent of American adults** Jamie Ballard, "Do Americans Believe in the Idea of Soulmates?," YouGov, February 10, 2021, accessed April 4, 2023, https://today.yougov.com/topics/society/articles-reports/2021/02/10/soulmates-poll-survey-data.

71 **"I had been in a healthy marriage"** Janet White to author, July 17, 2022.

72 **Republican Study Committee's (RSC) fiscal report** RSC, "Blueprint to Save America," July 6, 2022, accessed April 5, 2023, https://banks.house.gov/uploadedfiles/fy23_budget_final_copy.pdf.

72 **"greatest tool to lift women"** Annie Lowrey, "Can Marriage Cure Poverty?," *The New York Times,* February 4, 2014, accessed April 4, 2023, https://www.nytimes.com/2014/02/09/magazine/can-marriage-cure-poverty.html.

72   **There is research evidence that suggests** Sheila Kennedy, "Ideology, Inequality, and the Safety Net," Inequality.org, December 16, 2016, accessed April 4, 2023, https://inequality.org/research/shredding-social-safety-net/.

73   **"The number of marriages increases"** Misty Heggeness, "When Laws Make Divorce Easier, Research Shows Women Benefit, Outcomes Improve," U.S. Census Bureau, December 18, 2019, accessed April 4, 2023, https://www.census.gov/library/stories/2019/12/the-upside-of-divorce.html.

73   **In a TikTok that went viral** Jennifer Mock, "1950s Women Meet the Future," TikTok, September 9, 2022, accessed April 4, 2023, https://www.tiktok.com/@jlmock4.0/video/7138439107629305134.

74   **a wife is far more likely** "Scope of the Problem," VAWnet.

74   **stay-at-home moms are more likely to be depressed** Sharon Lerner, "Why Are Stay-at-Home Mothers More Depressed?," *Slate*, May 22, 2012, accessed April 4, 2023, https://slate.com/human-interest/2012/05/why-stay-at-home-mothers-are-more-depressed-than-working-moms.html.

74   **and anxious** Danielle Braff, "Being a Stay-at-Home Mom Is Not a Happy Job for Some," *Chicago Tribune*, July 15, 2016, accessed April 4, 2023, https://www.chicagotribune.com/lifestyles/parenting/sc-unhappy-stay-at-home-moms-family-0719-20160715-story.html.

74   **"It is more comfortable"** Simone de Beauvoir, *The Second Sex* (New York: Vintage, 2011).

4   Why Should I Change My Name?

80   **"I read in a book once"** Lucy Maud Montgomery, *Anne of Green Gables* (Boston: L. C. Page, 1908).

81   **"By rehearsing these clumsy"** Hermina Ibarra, "Provisional Selves: Experimenting with Image and Identity in Professional Adaptation," *Working Knowledge,* Harvard Business School, February 1, 2000, accessed April 4, 2023, https://hbswk.hbs.edu/archive/provisional-selves-experimenting-with-image-and-identity-in-professional-adaptation.

83   **The figures are imprecise because** Kristen Rogers, "Why Women Do or Don't Change Their Name When They Get Married," CNN, July 19, 2022, accessed April 4, 2023, https://edition

.cnn.com/2022/07/19/health/last-name-change-marriage-reasons
-wellness/.

83 **"It is quite surprising"** Maddy Savage, "Why Do Women Still
Change Their Names?," BBC, September 23, 2020, accessed
April 4, 2023, https://www.bbc.com/worklife/article/20200921
-why-do-women-still-change-their-names.

83 **For centuries when communities** Paul Blake, "What's in a
Name? Your Link to the Past," BBC, April 26, 2011, accessed
April 4, 2023, https://www.bbc.co.uk/history/familyhistory/get
_started/surnames_01.shtml.

84 **"The aim of the system"** Agnès Fine, Christiane Klapisch-
Zuber, and Siân Reynolds, "Editorial: The Naming of Women,"
Clio. Women, Gender, History 45 (2017): 7–32.

84 **But not everyone complied** Ibid.

85 **In 1855, when the feminist activist Lucy Stone** Debra Mi-
chals, "Lucy Stone," National Women's History Museum, 2017,
accessed April 9, 2023, https://www.womenshistory.org/education
-resources/biographies/lucy-stone#.

85 **Even in this century, women report** Leslie Mann, "Name
Change Can Alter the Course of Person's Life," *The Columbus
Dispatch,* September 19, 2017, accessed April 4, 2023, https://eu
.dispatch.com/story/lifestyle/2017/09/19/name-change-can-alter
-course/18781714007/.

85 **In 1971, Kathleen Harney, a Milwaukee** Gretchen Schuld,
"Unsung Legal Heroes: Kathleen Rose Harney and Joan Kessler;
Assistance from Ruth Bader Ginsburg," Wisconsin Justice Initiative, July 19, 2021, accessed April 4, 2023, https://www.wjiinc
.org/blog/unsung-legal-heroes-kathleen-rose-harney-and-joan
-kessler-assistance-from-ruth-bader-ginsburg.

87 **In a study on name changing** Brian Powell, Laura Hamilton,
and Claudia Geist, "Marital Name Change as a Window into
Gender Attitudes," *Gender and Society* 25, no. 2 (2011): 145–75.

89 **"In some cases, 'choice' is used"** Moira Donegan, "Hard
Choices," *Not the Fun Kind,* September 14, 2022, accessed April
4, 2023, https://moiradonegan.substack.com/p/hard-choices.

90 **"Patriarchal masculinity"** bell hooks, *All About Love* (New
York: William Morrow, 2018).

90 **"Despite the fact that my kids' names"** Aubrey Hirsch, "It's
2022 and People Are Still Confused That My Kids Have Their

Mother's Last Name," *Time*, February 4, 2022, accessed April 4, 2023, https://time.com/6143476/baby-with-mothers-last-name/.

92   **In *Inequalities of Love*** Averil Y. Clarke, *Inequalities of Love: College-Educated Black Women and the Barriers to Romance and Family* (Durham, N.C.: Duke University Press, 2011).

94   **Companies that call us family** Benjamin Artz, Amanda Goodall, and Andrew J. Oswald, "Research: Women Ask for Raises as Often as Men, but Are Less Likely to Get Them," *Harvard Business Review*, June 25, 2018.

94   **A *Glamour* survey** Paulette Perhach, "Why You—Yes, You—Need a F*ck-Off Fund," *Glamour*, April 23, 2018, accessed April 9, 2023, https://www.glamour.com/story/why-you-need-a-fuck-off-fund.

5   The Heterosexual Repair Project

98   **But it wasn't until the 1980s** Rose Eveleth, "Forty Years Ago, Women Had a Hard Time Getting Credit Cards," *Smithsonian Magazine*, January 8, 2014, accessed April 4, 2023, https://www.forbes.com/advisor/credit-cards/when-could-women-get-credit-cards/.

98   **Women earn less than men** "The Gender Gap: Women Pay More for Their Mortgage Than Men," OwnUp, September 14, 2021, accessed April 4, 2023, https://resources.ownup.com/women-pay-more-for-their-mortgage-than-men.

99   **"In New York and the northern New Jersey"** Ira Katznelson and Suzanne Mettler, "On Race and Policy History: A Dialogue About the G.I. Bill," *Perspectives on Politics* 6, no. 3 (2008): 519–37.

99   **Today, disparities in home appraisals** Anna Bahney, "The Black Homeownership Rate Is Now Lower Than It Was a Decade Ago," CNN, February 25, 2022, accessed April 4, 2023, https://edition.cnn.com/2022/02/25/homes/us-black-homeownership-rate/.

104 **A woman who runs a Facebook group** Emma Johnson, interview with Lyz Lenz, October 12, 2022.

107 **"To the extent to which women"** Elizabeth Spelman, *Repair: The Impulse to Restore in a Fragile World* (Boston: Beacon Press, 2003).

108 **like *The Atlantic*, where Arthur Brooks** Arthur C. Brooks,

"Marriage Is a Team Sport," *The Atlantic,* November 10, 2022, accessed April 9, 2023, https://www.theatlantic.com/family/archive/2022/11/how-collaboration-can-improve-marriage-relationships/672048/.

109 **women carry the majority of the cognitive load** Allison Daminger, "The Cognitive Dimension of Household Labor," *American Sociological Review* 84, no. 4 (2019), https://journals.sagepub.com/doi/10.1177/0003122419859007.

6   The Easy Way Out

119 **divorcing couples should be required to attend mandatory counseling** Beverly Willitt, "Room for Debate: When Divorce Is a Family Affair," *The New York Times,* February 13, 2013, accessed April 9, 2023, https://www.nytimes.com/roomfordebate/2013/02/13/when-divorce-is-a-family-affair.

119 **Most states have waiting periods** Kimberly Hiss, "If You Need a Divorce, These States Are the Fastest . . . and the Slowest," *Reader's Digest,* November 4, 2022, accessed April 9, 2023, https://www.rd.com/article/fastest-and-slowest-states-for-divorce/.

119 **Also, most marriage licenses** Alyssa Nekritz, "Love (and Marriage) Is in the . . . Courthouse," National Center for State Courts, February 14, 2023, accessed April 9, 2023, https://www.ncsc.org/information-and-resources/trending-topics/trending-topics-landing-pg/love-and-marriage-is-in-the-courthouse.

119 **Mississippi is one of two states without** Geoff Pender, "Divorce in Mississippi Difficult, Costly," *Clarion Ledger,* February 18, 2017, accessed April 9, 2023, https://eu.clarionledger.com/story/news/politics/2017/02/18/divorce-antiquated-laws/97862130/.

120 **In fact, even though some states** "Child Marriage in the United States," Equality Now, accessed April 9, 2023, https://www.equalitynow.org/learn_more_child_marriage_us/.

120 **And in the United States, while child** David McClendon and Aleksandra Sandstrom, "Child Marriage Is Rare in the U.S., Though This Varies by State," Pew Research Center, November 1, 2016, accessed April 9, 2023, https://www.pewresearch.org/fact-tank/2016/11/01/child-marriage-is-rare-in-the-u-s-though-this-varies-by-state/.

123 **In 2022, *New York Times* columnist** Tish Harrison Warren, "I

Married the Wrong Person, and I'm So Glad I Did," *The New York Times,* June 5, 2022, accessed April 9, 2023, https://www.nytimes .com/2022/06/05/opinion/marriage-satisfaction-love.html.

124 **A 2002 study argued** Linda Waite et al., "Does Divorce Make People Happy?," Research Gate, January 2002, accessed April 9, 2023, https://www.researchgate.net/publication/237233376_Does _Divorce_Make_People_Happy_Findings_From_a_Study_of _Unhappy_Marriages.

124 **Yet, a 2005 study suggests** Seb Walker, "Divorce Makes Women Happier than Men." *The Guardian,* July 4, 2005, accessed April 9, 2023, https://www.theguardian.com/society/2005/jul/04/ genderissues.uknews.

124 **One study that looked** Neal J. Roese and Amy Summerville, "What We Regret Most . . . and Why," *Personality and Social Psychology Bulletin* 31, no. 9 (2005): 1273–85, https://doi.org/10 .1177/0146167205274693.

127 **It's women, and women of color especially** Anne Helen Petersen, "Other Countries Have Social Safety Nets. The U.S. Has Women," *Culture Study,* November 11, 2020, accessed April 9, 2023, https://annehelen.substack.com/p/other-countries-have -social-safety.

127 **It's worth pointing out** Claire Cain Miller, "Nearly Half of Men Say They Do Most of the Home Schooling. 3 Percent of Women Agree," *The New York Times,* May 6, 2020, accessed April 9, 2023, https://www.nytimes.com/2020/05/06/upshot/pandemic -chores-homeschooling-gender.html.

127 **Add in the fact that husbands** Elsa Vulliamy, "Husbands 'Create Extra Seven Hours of Housework a Week,'" *The Independent,* February 20, 2016, accessed April 24, 2023, https://www .independent.co.uk/life-style/husbands-create-extra-seven-hours -of-housework-a-week-a6885951.html.

128 **"noticing, acknowledging, and empathizing"** Arlie Hochschild, *The Time Bind: When Work Becomes Home and Home Becomes Work* (New York: Henry Holt, 2001).

131 **"I only know that I will never again"** Elissa Schappell and Claudia Brodsky Lacour, "Toni Morrison, The Art of Fiction, No. 134," *The Paris Review* 128 (Fall 1993), accessed April 9, 2023, https://www.theparisreview.org/interviews/1888/the-art-of -fiction-no-134-toni-morrison.

131 **"it isn't brave to sit passively in your misery"** Rebecca Woolf, *All of This* (New York: HarperOne, 2022).

132 **"a conventional route that calcified"** Thessaly La Force, "When Two Artists Meet, and Then Marry," *The New York Times Style Magazine,* May 20, 2021, accessed April 9, 2023, https://www.nytimes.com/2021/05/20/t-magazine/artist-marriage-albers.html.

133 **In 1993, *Time* magazine published** Amitai Etzioni, "How to Make Marriage Matter," *Time,* September 6, 1993, accesssed April 24, 2023, https://content.time.com/time/subscriber/article/0,33009,979157,00.html.

7   The Revenge Dress

148 **"an inferior form of discourse"** Tressie McMillan Cottom, "Why We Should Talk About What Kyrsten Sinema Is Wearing," *The New York Times,* October 29, 2021, accessed April 9, 2023, https://www.nytimes.com/2021/10/29/opinion/sinema-vest-senate.html.

150 **Today, this advice is veiled** Matthew Hussey, "How to Be Confident When You Don't Feel Attractive," How to Get the Guy, September 18, 2022, accessed April 9, 2023, https://www.howtogettheguy.com/blog/how-to-be-confident-when-you-dont-feel-attractive/.

151 **"To be overly gendered about it"** Virginia Sole-Smith, "Do I Wear Spanx to Family Court?," *Burnt Toast,* November 1, 2022, accessed April 9, 2023, https://virginiasolesmith.substack.com/p/spanx-in-family-court.

8   Sex After Jesus

157 **When I was getting married, this statistic** Olga Khazan, "Fewer Sex Partners Means a Happier Marriage," *The Atlantic,* October 22, 2018, accessed April 9, 2023, https://www.theatlantic.com/health/archive/2018/10/sexual-partners-and-marital-happiness/573493/.

157 **Institute for Family Studies** Miranda Blue, "Meet the Anti-Gay Foundation Behind the Utah World Congress of Families," Right Wing Watch, October 28, 2015, accessed April 9, 2023, https://www.rightwingwatch.org/post/meet-the-anti-gay-foundation-behind-the-utah-world-congress-of-families/.

157 **A 2009 study found** Debby Herbenick et al., "Sexual Behavior

in the United States: Results from a National Probability Sample of Men and Women Ages 14–94," *The Journal of Sexual Medicine* 7, no. 5 (2010): 255–65.

157 **A 2017 study found a similar gap** David A. Frederick et al., "Differences in Orgasm Frequency Among Gay, Lesbian, Bisexual, and Heterosexual Men and Women in a U.S. National Sample," *Archives of Sexual Behavior* 47, no. 1 (2018): 273–88.

158 **Additionally, while 50 percent or more** Amanda Chatel, "More Than Half of Women Orgasm Through Oral Sex—but Most Aren't Receiving It," *Bustle,* September 14, 2018, accessed April 9, 2023, https://www.bustle.com/p/more-than-half -of-women-orgasm-through-oral-sex-but-most-arent-receiving-it -11910798.

158 **Women are twice as likely** Jessica Wood et al., "Was It Good for You Too? An Analysis of Gender Differences in Oral Sex Practices and Pleasure Ratings Among Heterosexual Canadian University Students," *The Canadian Journal of Sexuality* 25, no. 1 (2016): 21–29.

158 **"Men may think receiving oral sex"** Hui Liu, Shannon Shen, and Ning Hsieh, "A National Dyadic Study of Oral Sex, Relationship Quality, and Well-Being Among Older Couples," *The Journals of Gerontology: Series B* 74, no. 2 (2018): 298–308.

158 **In response to the news that rates of loneliness** Magdalene J. Taylor, "Have More Sex, Please!," *The New York Times,* February 13, 2023, accessed April 9, 2023, https://www.nytimes .com/2023/02/13/opinion/have-more-sex-please.html.

159 **This refusal is happening in the context** Donna St. George, "Teen Girls 'Engulfed' in Violence and Trauma, CDC Finds," *The Washington Post,* February 13, 2023, accessed April 9, 2023, https://www.washingtonpost.com/education/2023/02/13/teen-girls -violence-trauma-pandemic-cdc/.

159 **happening as the wage gap persists** Arwa Mahdawi, "One in Three Men Thinks Feminism Does More Harm Than Good. Surprise, Surprise," *The Guardian,* March 5, 2022, accessed April 9, 2023, https://www.theguardian.com/commentisfree/2022/mar/05/ week-in-patriarchy-feminism-arwa-mahdawi.

168 **"Our childhood is preparation"** Mariarosa Dalla Costa and Selma James, *The Power of Women and the Subversion of the Community,* 3rd ed. (Bristol, UK: Falling Wall Press, 1975).

9   #NotAllMen

177 **"'It's not hard not to be terrible'"** Garth Greenwell, "A Moral Education: In Praise of Filth," *Yale Review,* March 20, 2023, accessed April 9, 2023, https://yalereview.org/article/garth-greenwell -philip-roth.

182 **And while American mothers are far more likely** "Today's Parents Spend More Time with Their Kids Than Moms and Dads Did 50 Years Ago," UCI News, September 28, 2016, accessed April 9, 2023, https://news.uci.edu/2016/09/28/todays-parents -spend-more-time-with-their-kids-than-moms-and-dads-did-50 -years-ago/.

182 **A survey of Harvard Business School** Robin J. Ely, Pamela Stone, and Colleen Ammerman, "Rethink What You 'Know' About High-Achieving Women," *Harvard Business Review,* December 2014, accessed April 9, 2023, https://hbr.org/2014/12/rethink -what-you-know-about-high-achieving-women.

182 **One study found that women in Australia** Robert Breunig and Yinjunji Zhang, "Gender Norms and Domestic Abuse: Evidence from Australia," *Tax and Transfer Policy Institute,* March 2021, https://taxpolicy.crawford.anu.edu.au/sites/default/files/ publication/taxstudies_crawford_anu_edu_au/2021-04/complete _breunig_zhang_wp_mar_2021.pdf.

182 **nearly half of men with children** Miller, "Nearly Half of Men."

183 **In 2021, labor reports showed** Stephanie Ferguson, "Data Deep Dive: A Decline of Women in the Workforce," U.S. Chamber of Commerce, April 27, 2022, accessed April 9, 2023, https:// www.uschamber.com/workforce/data-deep-dive-a-decline-of -women-in-the-workforce.

183 **Birth rates are dropping** Cara Tabachnick, "U.S. Birth Rates Drop as Women Wait to Have Babies," CBS News, January 12, 2023, accessed April 9, 2023, https://www.cbsnews.com/news/u-s -birth-rate-decline-national-center-for-health-statistics-report/.

186 **"Love is the practice of freedom"** bell hooks, *Outlaw Culture: Resisting Representation* (New York: Routledge, 2006).

10   Marriage Is a Joke

192 **The origin of that joke** Mervyn Rothstein, "Henny Youngman, King of the One-Liners, Is Dead at 91 After 6 Decades of

Laughter," *The New York Times,* February 25, 1998, accessed
April 9, 2023, https://www.nytimes.com/1998/02/25/arts/henny
-youngman-king-of-the-one-liners-is-dead-at-91-after-6-decades
-of-laughter.html.

192 **When Jerry Seinfeld says** Stephen Armstrong, "Jerry Seinfeld:
Heard the One About the Reunion?," *The Guardian,* October 12,
2009, https://www.theguardian.com/media/2009/oct/12/jerry
-seinfeld-interview-comedy.

193 **Study after study shows that** Christie Nicholson, "The Humor
Gap," *Scientific American,* October 1, 2012, accessed April 9,
2023, https://www.scientificamerican.com/article/the-humor-gap
-2012-10-23/.

194 **"humor was more often misremembered"** Amanda Marcotte,
"Men Aren't Funnier Than Women but We'll Keep Pretending They
Are," *Slate,* October 20, 2011, accessed April 9, 2023, https://slate
.com/human-interest/2011/10/study-shows-that-men-aren-t-funnier
-than-women-but-that-people-generally-believe-that-they-are.html.

194 **researchers at Western University** Ibid.

194 **Humor in women is not often** Eric Bressler and Sigal
Balshine, "The Influence of Humor on Desirability," *Evolution
and Human Behavior* 27, no. 1 (2006): 29–39, accessed April 24,
2023, https://doi.org/10.1016/j.evolhumbehav.2005.06.002.

195 **"throw off the shackles of self-ridicule"** Naomi Weisstein,
"Why We Aren't Laughing Anymore," *Ms.,* November 1973,
49–51, 88–90.

11   The Bachelorette Party

210 **"There's no mistaking that divorce"** Lah Kyung, "Divorce
Ceremonies Give Japanese Couples a New Way to Untie the
Knot," CNN, September 7, 2010, accessed April 9, 2023, http://
edition.cnn.com/2010/WORLD/asiapcf/09/07/japan.divorce
.ceremonies/index.html.

210 **In the Beidane communities** Saied Zarbeea, "Inside the Lavish
Divorce Parties of the Beidane People," *Vice,* November 27, 2017,
accessed April 9, 2023, https://www.vice.com/en/article/ne3pyg/
inside-the-lavish-divorce-parties-of-beidane-people.

210 **"The congratulations of her friends"** "Divorce Party Is Latest
Fad," *St. Louis Post-Dispatch,* October 16, 1902.

210 **In 1912, the *San Francisco Chronicle*** Helen Dare, "Can Re-

verse 'Em for Celebrating Divorce—Now That Divorcees Make It Social Event," *San Francisco Chronicle,* October 11, 1912.

211 **"All of our big life transitions"** Christine Gallagher, "Experience: I'm a Divorce Party Planner," *The Guardian,* August 25, 2017, accessed April 9, 2023, https://www.theguardian.com/lifeandstyle/2017/aug/25/experience-divorce-party-planner.

212 **The Chippendales website** "Divorcée," Chippendales Divorce Party Packages, June 23, 2022, accessed March 30, 2023, https://web.archive.org/web/20220623035235/https://chippendales.com/girls-night/divorc%C3%A9e.

213 **"Where hearts are broken"** Kimberly Long, "A Divorce Liturgy?," *Pray Tell* (blog), August 3, 2018, accessed April 9, 2023, https://www.praytellblog.com/index.php/2018/08/03/a-divorce-liturgy/.

12   Finding the Night Sky

218 **In a 2022 article for *Slate*** Gail Cornwall and Scott Coltrane, "How Americans Became Convinced Divorce Is Bad for Kids," *Slate,* July 11, 2022, accessed April 9, 2023, https://slate.com/technology/2022/07/divorce-bad-for-kids-history.html.

13   Burning the Dress

236 **In her novel *Heartburn*** Nora Ephron, *Heartburn* (New York: Alfred A. Knopf, 1983).

238 **In 2022, musician Kaya Nova** Kaya Nova (@thekayanova), "People think they're competing with other suitors," Twitter, July 14, 2021, 10:36 A.M., accessed April 9, 2023, https://twitter.com/thekayanova/status/1415334512356122624?lang=en.

244 **women feel compelled to do more** Rebecca Macatee, "Single Moms Spend Less Time on Chores, and Married Moms Are Frankly Not Surprised," *Parents,* May 14, 2019, accessed April 9, 2023, https://www.parents.com/news/single-moms-spend-less-time-on-chores-and-married-moms-are-not-surprised/.

About the Author

LYZ LENZ is a journalist and the author of *God Land* and *Belabored*. She has written for *Insider, The New York Times, Marie Claire,* and *The Washington Post*. Lenz also writes the newsletter *Men Yell at Me,* about the intersection of politics and personhood in red-state America. She lives in Iowa with her two children.

About the Type

This book was set in Fairfield, the first typeface from the hand of the distinguished American artist and engraver Rudolph Ruzicka (1883–1978). Ruzicka was born in Bohemia (in the present-day Czech Republic) and came to America in 1894. He set up his own shop, devoted to wood engraving and printing, in New York in 1913 after a varied career working as a wood engraver, in photoengraving and banknote printing plants, and as an art director and freelance artist. He designed and illustrated many books, and was the creator of a considerable list of individual prints—wood engravings, line engravings on copper, and aquatints.